Wisconsin Hills Farm Stories

Wisconsin Hills
Farm Stories

Adventures of a Biodynamic Farmer

MARIE-LAURE VALANDRO

Portal Books

2012

Portal Books

128 Second Place, Brooklyn, New York 11231

Library of Congress Cataloging-in-Publication Data is Available

ISBN: 978-1-938685-02-6

Contents

Preface

The beings of the elemental kingdom—the gnomes, undines, sylphs, salamanders—help build up and form the plants. These beings were led and influenced by certain higher beings who are now withdrawing from this activity, just as at certain times these higher beings withdraw their influence within human beings and apply themselves to higher tasks. The elemental spirits are thus left to themselves, and other spirits (Lucifer, Ahriman) seize them and draw them away from their work in forming the plants. The result will be a diminution of the spiritual forces of the plants and a gradual general atrophy, against which artificial fertilizers will not help.

What must now be striven for is that human beings familiarize themselves with the elemental kingdom, and that they attempt to come in connection with these elemental spirits. In a sense, human beings must take over and prevent other powers from using the elemental kingdom and must strive to influence these spirits in such a way that they continue to assist the growth of plants.

If human beings are able to cultivate these kinds of forces in themselves, they will become priests as farmers. If it is not possible to bring about such a connection, then in a few decades human beings will have to experience that the yield and quality of the products of the fields are diminishing and that no remedy can be found.

The undines take part in the formation of the dew. These spirits too are on the verge of being drawn away from their previous activities by other beings. In time this would have the consequence that the formation of dew would gradually cease. Here, too, human beings must strive to bring influence to bear.

A further task for human beings is to live consciously with the rhythm of the seasons (namely, to experience nature in spring through the physical body, in summer through the ether body, in autumn through the astral body, and in winter through the "I"). With such an attitude, a spring planting, for example, will have a completely different mood than that of an autumn planting.

In order to gain a spiritual relationship to the animal kingdom, the human being must penetrate to the group souls of the animal genera. One can already perceive—and this will increase significantly—that the instincts of the animals are becoming weaker. For example, animals will no longer avoid poisonous foods in their fodder, but will instead eat them along with the rest.

> When human beings penetrate to the group souls, they can then compensate, for example, for the weakening of the animals' instincts; the animals can thereby be helped.[1]

To practice these words by Rudolf Steiner, I bought a farm. Farming has proved to be no easy task, but one that is needed in our modern world. This book is the product of this adventure and is meant to help farmers and gardeners understand some of the beautiful words from Steiner and others, who remind us of the important tasks we face in the future. They join food for thought with food for the stomach.

> For in very truth, every single thing in the universe is a written character if we could but read it."[2]

> ... You may be a painter and have mastered the art of painting up to a point. When you become an anthroposophist, you will find that the influences of which I am speaking flow into the way you instinctively master the art. You find it easier to mix your colours, and the ideas you want come more readily. Or let us assume you are an academic person and supposed to do some scientific work. Many who are in this situation will know how much effort it often takes to collect the literature needed to solve some particular problem. When you become an anthroposophist you will no longer go to libraries and first of

1. Rudolf Steiner, *Agriculture: Spiritual Foundations for the Renewal of Agriculture* (Kimberton, PA: Bio-Dynamic Farming and Gardening Association, 1993), pp. 254–255.

2. Rudolf Steiner, *Harmony of the Creative Word: The Human Being and the Elemental, Animal, Plant, and Mineral Kingdoms* (London: Rudolf Steiner Press, 2001), p. 33.

all borrow fifty volumes that are of no use, which is what you did before; instead, you will immediately lay your hands on the book you want. Spiritual science has a direct influence on your life; it changes your instincts and gives new mainsprings to life that make you more skillful in life.[3]

It mattered enormously to Rudolf Steiner that anthroposophic knowledge should not remain merely in the ego, but that it should be *taken inside* to encompass the soul, the middle sphere of the human being at its deepest. Therefore he once described what he regarded as the real beginning of the anthroposophic movement in the following way....

The moment that souls feel like bursting with rapture and are thrilled with joy at one or another aspect of some especially important truth, only then and not before, in such people as feel themselves to be anthroposophists, is the anthroposophic movement born. It is born; it really begins to exist as anthroposophic movement only in the whole human being.... How far, here and now, are we capable of catching fire within and rejoicing in sheer rapture at anthroposophic ideas? Then, from this point of view, just think about the beginning of the anthroposophic movement.[4]

3. Rudolf Steiner, *The Inner Nature of Man and Life Between Death and Rebirth*, Lecture in Vienna April 12, 1914 (Bristol: Rudolf Steiner Press, 1994), p. 111.

4. Maria Roschl-Lehrs, *The Second Man in Us* (Canterbury, UK: Henry Goulden Books, 1977), p. 17.

Writing this story was not planned, but just happened like much else in my life. Nonetheless, I hope that many readers will become enthusiastic about farm life and move to a small piece of land, no matter how small—somewhere, anywhere. Do it with the intent to enjoy our Earth and love and preserve it with enthusiasm for the future, to be in God.

Farm Stories
Spring & Summer 2007–2008

WHAT A GREAT RELIEF! We just finished haying the thirty-acre alfalfa-timothy grass field. It is all chaotically stacked, pell-mell in the big barn. We do not have enough help to do otherwise, as the conveyor belt that runs from the tractor's PTO (power take-off shaft) throws the bales into the barn. At least it is there, ready for our animals this winter. We have three cows, one bull, two mares, a young stallion, an Arab gelding, fifteen sheep, one beautiful ram with nice horns, and a flock of fifty chickens with three roosters to serve them. I sat on the big forty-year-old tractor, pulling the hay combine with a wagon attached to it, which collects the small bales of hay. It looks big—it is big—and I know nothing about machines. I just drive them carefully, watch for problems, and hope that all works well.

The sky today was a deep indigo with large cumulus clouds boding ominous weather, and I still had several rows of hay to collect. I mentally repeated to our friends, the clouds: Please, not now—just another hour and I will be

Unloading hay with a 50-year-old tractor

finished. Then you can drop your blessed water on the land! Lo and behold the rain came, a few drops at first, just before I finished. My son hastily moved the hay bales into the barn, feeding them to the pulley system. By eight o'clock that evening we had finished.

Every year in late May and early June, farmers go through this painful process, waiting for a window of good weather to cut the hay, a window which never seems to come. We cut the hay and it was rained on, although we were lucky and it dried the next day. Sometimes farmers lose a whole field and must face the prospect of buying hay for their animals. But for us, this time, we give a deep sigh of thankfulness since we have enough at least for the next few months. The second cutting will be in early August when the weather is usually better. But here in the Midwest that is also the time of tornadoes, which can loom suddenly on the horizon and we know trouble is coming. It is also a time when I make fantastic photos, with dark indigo in the background and beautiful bright orange and yellow flower gardens in the foreground.

I remember when we first moved here. One afternoon we were moving our things to the new farm we are on today, and I had left my ten-year-old daughter at another farm just ten miles away to pack up her things. My son was on the roof of the new farmhouse, fixing it. We saw dark clouds on the southwestern horizon where the other farm was and I knew something was up. As I drove back to fetch my daughter, I saw uprooted trees and fields that had been totally flattened. When I arrived at the old place my daughter was relieved to see me. She said she had heard a big hissing sound and had run into the basement, because it started to blow very hard. The tornado had come right through the farm, between the barn and the house, leaving them intact. We could plainly see its path as it had uprooted several large oaks.

I was very happy to find my daughter safe and that she had the presence of mind to have gone into the basement. We had just moved a year earlier from New Hampshire, where we had never experienced tornadoes, just windy storms. Welcome to the Midwest.

We love the new farm, though we miss hiking in New England. We had, however, grown a bit weary of never seeing the sunrise there, as it was always hidden by tall trees, forests, or mountains. Our new home in Wisconsin has 360-degree views of sunrises, sunsets, and magnificent shows of light and darkness. For me as a painter, it is heavenly. The sky is immense, with great always-moving clouds, and at night it is dark, very dark, often with a beautiful show of stars. Here we also have the animals, plants, and earth to care for, to learn from, and to meditate on.

By about mid-April, the work begins here on the farm. One must prepare the gardens of perennials, herbs, and vegetables, as well as the flowforms and the pond with its little waterfall, which need to be cleaned and the pumps reinstalled. It is never-ending work from early morning until late at night. Meanwhile, the animals need to be fed and the chicken coop cleaned to prepare it for spring, when all the broody chickens must sit on their eggs.

Now there is only my husband and me on this farm. My son comes to give us a hand around May, and this year he is with us to help with another project as well. He usually fixes everything that my husband and I have broken during the year—the old trucks, lawn mowers, tractors, machinery, and other equipment. We love this farm, but we are not farmers. We both have other jobs: I paint and write and he is a physician in a busy Milwaukee hospital. Nonetheless, we enjoy living on a farm with all that it entails. We would not change it, even though there is never a time when we can truly say that everything is finished. It never is. We have learned to say, "That is enough for today; we will continue tomorrow, and the next day." We make time to stop working and take a bike ride or go horseback riding. This continues until the first week in October.

This year I was away from the farm from late April to early May and missed picking dandelion flowers for our biodynamic preparation. The fields surrounding the farm are full of dandelions that look like they are smiling at the sky. They seem happy to show up, and they grow with tremendous speed. The neighbors happily spray them, disliking their happy little faces on their perfect green lawns. The dandelion-green salads are excellent for one's health. The French know and adore the *pissenlit* as beneficial for problematic liver complaints.

Taraxacum, the dandelion ... the innocent, yellow dandelion (*dent de lion*) is a tremendous asset, because it mediates between fine homeopathic distribution of silicic acid in the cosmos, and the silicic acid that is actually used over the whole region. The dandelion is really a kind of messenger from heaven. But if we need this plant and want to make it effective in the manure, we have to utilize it in the right way. It must be exposed, to the Earth's influence, to the Earth's winter influence.... Collect the yellow heads of the dandelion and let them wilt a little. Then pack them together and sew them up in a bovine mesentery [abdominal tissue], and put them, too, in the earth through the winter. When these balls are dug up in the spring, they will in fact be thoroughly saturated with cosmic influence, and can be stored until needed. This material can be added to the manure in the same way as before, and it will give the soil the ability to attract just as much silicic acid from the atmosphere and from the cosmos as is needed by the plants. In this way the plants will become sensitive to everything at work in their environment and then be able to draw in whatever else they need....

Fertilizers of the future should not be prepared with all kinds of chemicals, but rather with yarrow, chamomile, nettle, oak bark, and dandelion. A fertilizer of this kind will in fact contain very much of what is actually needed."[5]

---

5. Steiner, *Agriculture,* p. 103.

Now, it is the first week in June and I have not planted the potatoes yet. This morning I planted zinnias, lots and lots of them, as well as cucumbers and zucchini. The lettuce, arugula, and radishes are coming along, planted too late because I was traveling and did not return home until May 10. My flower gardens need another week or so of full-time weeding and planting. Then I will work for only a couple of hours a day in the gardens or simply stroll through them. At that time I start full-time watercolor painting in my small studio, a former machinist shop. It is still full of the wonderful, creative energies of the two old brothers who I am told used to fix things there.

The month of June is a magical time for gardeners. It is the time of bearded irises and all sorts of wonderful spring plants that seemingly transform the gardens overnight from springtime brown, black, and beige into a symphony of colors and shapes. Although we witness this transformation every year, one never gets used to its magic. It is always a new experience, and then one says good-bye to these beautiful beings for another year. They make their appearances and then disappear. So I dutifully walk in my garden and say hello to whomever has bloomed overnight, trying not to forget anyone.

I have a large garden, so it takes quite a while to stroll through it to meet all these wonderful beings and acknowledge their presence. If sometimes I must be away for a few days, I can feel that my absence has been noticed. So I try to go away less frequently from the gardens during spring and summer, for there is no one else to see their beauty, and

Bearded irises in the garden

that hurts them. One must be attentive to all this beauty. During spring and summer, I become a servant of the plant kingdom. This is easy because I love them all, and the only way I can face the enormous amount of work needed to keep all these gardens thriving is to love them. The rewards are enormous. It is not just the beautiful colors and forms, but I also receive their great energies as I work closely with them. After I had been working with them a while, it occurred to me that I do not even need to eat some of these plants; just working with a plant is enough. By tending it I receive its wonderful healing energies. I have often told friends that if everyone in the world had a garden in their backyard we would not have wars. No one would be savage enough to destroy someone's gardens or orchards after knowing what it took to grow them.

I have also noticed that when someone comes to visit my garden I know immediately what kind of person that individual is. Some just walk quickly and see nothing; that tells me something. Others are full of questions, but never listen to the answers. Some take a plant and look at it with love. Some walk quietly, taking in everything, while others have no time for a garden at all. Characters are revealed in the process. As people treat a garden, so they treat themselves, their own life, and their friends.

On our farm, we have lots of gardens, bushes, and tall trees, and consequently we have many birds. They like the untreated fields. On the sunrise side of the farm, we have four large Chinese elm trees that offer us shade during the hot summer. On the southern side, we have a great-great-grandpa elm tree that shades my painting studio, the new gallery, and a therapy room. He is the oldest tree in our area. Though I have looked for a larger one, he wins. He, then, is the caretaker of at least a ten-mile radius, a magnificent tree requiring the arm spans of three men to circle his trunk. When we groom the horses, we usually tie them to his trunk, which they like. He has seen many storms rage in his 200+ years of life. The birds love this tree and always nest or rest there while surveying the surrounding area. We know we are under his protection as well.

Many red-winged blackbirds nest in the fields, and we also see bluebirds nesting on the fences. We can immediately spot the bright orange of the Oriole, and many yellow finches use my little pond garden as a huge birdbath. The chickens, of course, are all over the place, even where we do not want them, such as in the newly seeded bed of annuals. Hummingbirds come to the feeder and to plants in the gardens. The barn is home to many pigeons and doves dressed in rich grey tones. Crows are always chatting on the main road, which is not very busy, and the Native Americans say that this is a good sign and means that it is social time in the area. We also have the eagle family, which we may see trying to find a rabbit or one of my small chickens for lunch. Around five o'clock in the afternoon, the birds take a last-minute bath before returning to their nests. Meanwhile, the roosters are happily running from one hen to the other, who seem to say, "Don't ruffle my feathers again."

The frogs jump in the pond and hide from the chickens, while Aris, our German shepherd, relaxes lazily on the porch. In another hour it will be time to get up and bark all night at whatever moves. We have gotten used to it. In the morning, after a long night of work, he is exhausted and sleeps all day. While we sleep, Aris keeps guard and seems to take his job seriously. At night, the foxes and especially the coyotes come out to find food for their young, and my sheep would make a nice meal. Thanks to Aris, they keep away. His other pastime is running after the horse along the fence line, a game they both enjoy. Meanwhile, the year-old stallion is free to go wherever he wishes; he is not fenced in. So he visits his mother, his friend Silky, the mare, and two beautiful paint mares beyond the fence line, as well as his friend Max, the Arabian gelding beyond the other fence. When he gets bored, he challenges himself by jumping into the large horse trailer, where he stays until he gathers the courage to jump out again. My husband says that all these challenges make him smarter, and it is much better than tucking him away in a stall.

It is a hot, sticky day, and large cumulus clouds loom over the farm. We will have more rain, which will help our gardens, as well as the soy and corn fields throughout the region. This morning, I picked up a gallon of fresh milk from our local biodynamic farm and made butter with the cream. I also collected two dozen eggs, which our hens are now laying every day, providing me the challenge of selling them. I have too many eggs and no one to buy them. It costs too much to raise them and buy their organic food, which needs to be shipped from western Wisconsin, since we do not grow corn in the eastern part of the state. People are not willing to pay what it costs for me to raise these birds, so I face the hard fact that we have to butcher half of them. I love these little creatures and hate the fact that they will have to go. I have gone to friends but only a few buy the eggs; the rest prefer to buy cheap supermarket eggs. This is a shame because the eggs are beautiful and of excellent quality. We have cross-bred the chickens, and the eggs come in all colors—shades of turquoise, brown, beige, light and dark green. These are the realities of farming in the United States. I have to face the fact that I am not a businessperson or even a real farmer, but simply someone who loves the land. We grow things because we have the land and we are successful at it, but it is another thing to find a market for our produce. We must limit how many chickens we have and not let them sit happily on their eggs, although I love seeing the chicks.

❧

Since the weather is hot, I need to have a sheep shearer come to the farm soon. We sheared a few of them ourselves, but it took two hours for two animals. A friend of my son is a tall-ship sea captain, as is my son. His girlfriend came to visit and wanted to try shearing the sheep. They enjoyed it, but I think the sheep enjoyed it much less. One of them escaped half sheared and looked quite funny. Our professional sheep shearer can shear all the sheep in a couple of hours. He is a history teacher during the school year, and during the summer he does part-time sheep shearing with his older son. They are tall blond Norwegian men.

It is the weekend, and my neighbors are all mowing their lawns. Maintaining a perfectly mowed lawn is a ritual in Wisconsin as, indeed, it is in the whole United States. I did mine, too, but not to perfection. More clouds drifted in and out, giving us showers, dark sky, blue sky with large cumulus clouds, and then dark sky again. Today it is raining, grey, good for the gardens. I went out to water the horses, the sheep, the beautiful Black Angus cows, our one bull, and three other cows. The young stallion was ready for his oats. My son has gone to British Columbia for the summer and fall, and my husband will join him there every two weeks. I am the only one to take care of the farm duties, a responsibility for which I am not exactly cut out. The mare Silky is in heat, and the young stallion was up against the fence ready to do his business. I just need to let the mare out and have the stallion breed her, but I am quite nervous about this. These animals are so large, and I am not very tall. Managing such

Sheep shearing

an activity is beyond my powers and abilities. Perhaps Phil, our friend and veterinarian, can give me a hand.

I remember one day, a couple of years ago in the fall, my husband had brought in a bull from the neighbors' farm to breed with our cows but had forgotten to tell me. When I went to the barn that morning to feed and water them, there was a huge bull staring at me as I threw the bales of hay. I did not notice him at first and assumed he was one of the cows. But when I noticed that he did not have an udder, but dangling balls instead, I ran out of there quite fast. The boys always laugh at my cowardliness, which I would call a concern for safety. I think it is really more of a men-versus-women issue.

I love to work with plants, but animal husbandry is not my forte. I water the animals and give them bales of hay, but handling them is too much for me. When we first moved in and the fences were not quite established, the sheep ran all over the place. We had a very large, somewhat wild, ram at the time with a huge double set of horns. One morning as I was feeding the chickens, he chased me and I ran to hide in a small dilapidated shed, which he proceeded to butt with his strong horns. I thought that this was the end of my farm life, but after a long ten minutes, he went away. I ran into the farmhouse, still fearful he might go through the glass door. The next morning, my husband tied him up in the back of our pickup truck, and I had to drive him to the butcher's house to have him made into sausages. I thought he was going to escape from the truck onto the major highway. This was at seven o'clock in the morning.

Now all the animals are well fenced in, but the stallion could easily go through the fence, which is not very strong, at least not for a stallion although he is still quite young. I ride but never feel completely relaxed. When I was in my early twenties and living in Vermont, a horse I was riding fell on its side. Luckily, I didn't break anything, but now I am extremely cautious. I ride with no saddle, which makes it easier to jump off if something happens. I still love to ride, however, and would hate to give it up entirely.

The weeding is almost finished, though not perfectly. Now I need to clean out the studio and start painting. It is a good day for that since it is raining and I cannot work in the gardens anyway. After a few days of cold, this morning it is rainy and in the 50s.

A day later and I am happy to see the Sun, but it is not a pleasant warmth. The temperature climbs into the 90s in a matter of hours, and the winds are picking up to forty miles per hour, predicting severe weather and the possibility of tornadoes. I have to take care of all small items lying around, such as lawn furniture, and I am disappointed because I was going to plant a bed of my favorite plants: bells of Ireland. They will have to wait for tomorrow. The very warm wind is scaring the dog and he hides in the garage, making me a bit nervous. We have very large trees that shed their dead branches when the wind is strong, so I must stay out of the gardens altogether. My studio is ready for me to begin painting, but with this howling wind, I'd rather stay inside the farmhouse. There is too much movement for me to get into a meditative mood and work with watercolor veils. The great-great grandfather tree is right beside my studio, bending its enormous branches under the fierce, hot wind.

Life in the heartland is never boring. We don't have tall majestic mountains or great sandy beaches, although there are beaches on the great lakes, but the skies, the clouds, and the winds certainly make up for these things. Here we feel the strength of the elements every day. Between yesterday and today, there has been a change of 45 degrees. I will have to walk around the whole property to see if any trees have fallen on the fence. I do not want my cows, horses, and sheep wandering onto someone else's land. If there is a tree on the fence, it will have to wait until my husband comes home, because I cannot use the chain saw. I could learn, but I won't.

When the wind is screaming like this, it is a bit difficult to concentrate on my agenda. "It is time to listen to me," says brother wind. And we all do. It is a cleansing feeling, especially when the heavy rain arrives in the evening, doing its magic for the farms. Then I go from one window to another to watch the wild scenery, happy to be in a sturdy house that has stood strong since the 1850s. As compensation, the house is decorated with bouquets of many blossoms, including wild and domestic irises, peonies, and daisies.

Bells of Ireland in the garden

I decided to drive into town to check my e-mail at the small internet café and interior decorating store. This small town west of Milwaukee seems still in the 1950s. We have six bars and only one nice coffee shop. Because of the weather, everyone is on edge today. We can't make plans, but must sit and wait for the storm to pass through. It is a long day of watching the weather.

The large animals do not seem concerned about any kind of weather. They are out in the fields enjoying the fresh grass and the wind. The rain does not change a thing in their agenda—peacefully graze, graze, and graze some more. The cows, undisturbed, observe life quietly with huge brown eyes, soft and kind, their wet noses smelling the air, looking almost like gentle deer. These few words characterize my feelings about cows:

And now you will wonder even less that a religious world conception, which penetrates so deeply into the spiritual as does Hinduism, venerates the cow, for it is the animal which continually spiritualizes the earth and continually gives to the earth that spiritual substance which it has taken from the cosmos. And we really should allow the following image to become real in our minds: beneath a grazing herd of cattle, the earth is quickened to joyful vigorous life, and the elemental spirits down there rejoice because they are assured of their nourishment from the cosmos through the existence of the creatures grazing above them. And we ought to paint a picture of the dancing, rejoicing airy sphere of the elemental spirits hovering around the eagle. Then we would portray spiritual realities, and the physical would be seen within the spiritual realities; we would see the eagle extending outwards in his aura, and the rejoicing of the elemental air spirits and fire spirits of the air playing into that aura.

We would see that remarkable aura of the cow which is in such marked contrast to earthly existence; because it is entirely cosmic; we would see lively merriment in the senses of the elemental earth spirits, who are here able to perceive what they have lost by being constrained to live out their existence in the darkness of the earth. For these spirits, what appears in the cow is sun. The elemental spirits whose dwelling place is in the earth cannot rejoice in the physical sun, but they can rejoice in the astral bodies of the animals which chew the cud.[6]

In addition to their beauty, the cows on our farm give us their manure and keep the back fields trimmed and nutrient-rich. They eat all the shrubs and weeds as they wander, keeping a gentle watch over the land and finding favorite spots during the summer to stand in the shade of tall trees or by springs in the cool mud. Here is a more scientific, earthly view of the cow:

> *Cow manure* is the best manure that can be used for composting purposes, as is evident by examining the long, complicated digestive organism of this beast. Cud-chewing ruminants like the bison or buffalo made possible the humus-rich prairies, which became the bread basket of the world. Were it not for the sacred cows, India would be in much worse shape than it is. These cows are not competitors, as some Western technocrats believe, but they live in symbiosis with human beings, eating weeds and roughage that could not otherwise be utilized and returning milk, draft power and manure. The dung amounts to 700 million tons annually, half of which serves as fertilizer and the other half as fuel (the thermal equivalent of 27 million tons of kerosene, 35 million tons of coal, or 68 million tons of wood). In countries of the cooler latitudes, cows are one of the mainstays of fertility, because with high rainfall and low temperatures, the soils become leached and acidic, leading to podsols and peat formations. The

---

6. Steiner, *Harmony of the Creative Word,* pp. 51–52.

Beautiful manure

cows, inside their warm organisms carry a microbial flora and fauna that break down, ferment, and digest cellulose, proteins, carbohydrates and other such substances that might be done externally in the soil in the warmer latitudes, but here must be done inside the animal organism. The intestinal micro-organisms help to bind the nutrients into the manures so that fertility can come to the acidic, starved northern soils.

When one looks at the ruminants, one finds four-chambered stomachs. In the first two chambers, the rumen and the reticulum, chewed plant material is stored and fermented. Bacterial flora by the billions are involved in this pre-digestion. Fiber and roughage cause regurgitation of the food and a further chewing of the cud. Bacteria and protozoa secrete enzymes (cellulase) which break down the glucose-yielding cellulose. Complex acid-base relationships permeate the digestion process. Amino acids, vitamin B12, and fatty acids are synthesized by these microorganisms for the cow. No other animal can make such good use of roughage. Feeding grain, Peruvian sardines, and nitrogen-rich alfalfa to cattle is violating their basic nature and will make these animals sick (scuttles, milk fevers, etc.). The alimentary tract is richly endowed with nervous tissue, monitoring the digestive process the whole long distance of the alimentary canal. It takes 18 days for this process to be completed.

It is appropriate to compare the complexity of the cow's digestion to that of the human brain. Whereas in primate fashion our senses are turned outward to the world at large, the seemingly dull cow has its senses turned inward, into its digestion, "meditating" on the forces and energies that are fixed into the vegetable kingdom and liberating these forces during digestion. No wonder the cow is sacred in India, for besides its utilitarian uses, it is the very image of a consciousness turned inward upon itself in deepest meditation. With this in mind, is it any wonder that cow dung, cow manure, has a special healing value for the soil and makes the best compost material imaginable?

It is one of the greatest sins of our time to have severed the cows from the land and placed them into concentrated livestock operations, to have deprived the human being of his association with this beatific beast, and to have chemical salts replace their valuable manure.[7]

One of the main reasons we own a farm is to let these beautiful cows and bulls live freely in the pastures. Most farms in Wisconsin no longer have cows wandering in pastures. Thousands of cows are inside immense open barns, and the fields no longer rejoice in the presence of these wonderful beings. As quoted, the elemental beings no longer have their "Sun beings," the cows. One feels the abandonment of farms very strongly as one travels throughout the state. When one does see an old farm with cows in its fields, the feeling is altogether different. It is almost magical. Seeing an ultra-modern farm after experiencing an old farm, one really feels the devastation of the land. It is truly a shame and all the more reason for young people to move back to small farms and allow cows to roam in the meadows. Idealism aside, however, one must be prepared for the demands of farming—physically, psychologically, and spiritually. By keeping in mind the importance of such work, we are able to continue even when we no longer feel we have the strength to do so. I hope that writing these little anecdotes will help young farmers continue their work. Here is an insight into meditation and the work of the farmer:

> Let's ask ourselves what we are actually doing when we meditate. In the East, people used to do this in a particular way. We in the West, in Europe, do it differently. Our kind of meditation depends on the breathing process only indirectly; we live in the rhythm of concentration and meditation.

7. Wolf D. Storl, *Culture and Horticulture: A Philosophy of Gardening* (Wyoming, RI: Bio-Dynamic Literature, 1979), pp. 261–262.

Nevertheless, what we do by devoting ourselves to these soul exercises still has a bodily counterpart, even though it is very delicate and subtle. In a very subtle way, the regular pace of our breathing, which is so closely tied to human life, is always slightly changed during meditation. While meditating, we retain somewhat more carbon dioxide than we do in a state of normal waking consciousness. A little extra carbon dioxide always remains behind in us. Usually, we are eager to thrust the full force of carbon dioxide out into our surroundings, but in this case we hold some back. We don't thrust the full force of carbon dioxide out there, into the environment that is filled with nitrogen. We hold some back.

You see, if you bump your head against something hard—a table, for instance—you will be aware only of your own pain. If, however, you rub against it more gently, you will become aware of the surface of the table and so on. It is the same when you meditate. You gradually grow into an experience of the nitrogen that surrounds you. That is the real process involved in meditation. Everything becomes known, including everything that lives in nitrogen. And this nitrogen is a very smart fellow who can teach you about what Mercury and Venus and the rest of them are doing, because it knows these things and is sensitive to them. Activities like meditation are based on very real processes.

And, in fact, it is at this point that the spirit of our inner activity begins to acquire a certain relationship to farming. This interaction of our soul and spirit with everything that is around us is what has always particularly aroused the interest of our dear friend Stegemann [a farmer in the audience]. It is not a bad thing, you know, when a farmer can meditate and thus become ever more receptive to the revelations of nitrogen. Our agricultural practices gradually change once we become reflective to what nitrogen can reveal. Suddenly, we know all kinds of things; they are simply there. Suddenly we know all about the mysteries at work on the land and around the farm…. Take a simple farmer, someone an educated person would not consider educated. The educated person may say the farmer is stupid, but in fact that is not true, for the simple reason that the farmer is actually a meditator. The farmer meditates on many, many things during the winter nights and, indeed, arrives at a way of acquiring spiritual knowledge. The farmer is simply unable to express it. It just happens that knowledge is suddenly there. As the farmer walks through the fields, it's suddenly there. One knows something, and afterward tries it out….

Mere intellectuality is not enough; it does not get us deep enough. Nature's life and flow are so fine and subtle that, in the end, they slip right through the coarse mesh of our rational concepts. This is the mistake science has made in recent times. It tries to use coarse conceptual nets to catch things that are actually much too fine for them.[8]

---

8. Steiner, *Agriculture,* pp. 55–56.

❧

Last night, severe thunderstorms hit our area just before eleven o'clock. I was in bed and had to go downstairs to safer ground. Right before my eyes, I observed a cold front meet a warm front, with enormously powerful lightening and thunder on all sides, and howling wind swirling the branches of the tall trees. Here is an insight into lightening:

> Think for a moment whither the water evaporates— it rises and reaches higher and higher into the region of the spiritual; it moves away from matter empty of spirits here below and rises into the spiritual world above. It is actually spirit that produces what looks like our electric spark. For, as we rise, we move higher and higher into the regions of the spiritual. Matter is present only in proximity to the earth. Higher up, it is surrounded by the spirit. Therefore, at the moment when the water vapor rises and reaches the region of the spiritual, the flash is produced. The water first becomes more spiritual- ized and then it falls again, "densified."[9]

Through all this, I listened to our weather radio, which most farmers in our area keep handy. It gives up-to-date weather reports on the exact location of tornadoes and how quickly the weather system is moving. I knew from listen- ing that the storm was directly above the farm and moving in a northeasterly direction, with wind gusts up to seventy

9. Rudolf Steiner, *Learning to See into the Spiritual World: Lectures to the Workers at the Goetheanum* (Great Barrington, MA: Steiner- Books/Anthroposophic Press, 1990, 2009), p. 73.

miles an hour. Then, after great winds, lightening bolts, and explosions of thunder, the downpour began, making it impossible to see much out the window. Everything was an eerie gray, owing to an almost full moon. It looked like the ocean was in the air. I was hoping that the animals would be well, since most of them stay outside. One hears that occasionally livestock are struck by lightening. Then after about forty-five minutes, the storm subsided and the winds died down to forty-five miles per hour or so. I went back to sleep.

The weather now is much cooler, about sixty-five degrees. Again I think that people living in this area must feel very secure and confident, with their feet firmly planted on the ground, because the weather certainly is a challenge. It is exhausting to live through such volatile weather.

How do the frail flowers always survive? Already all is back to normal. I watch the little hummingbird come to the feeder while I eat my breakfast.

A friend calls to invite me for strawberry picking at our veggie co-op. People in town are much lighter today, following yesterday's palpable tension. It is cool and very pleasant to sit among the strawberry patches and smell their delightful aroma. Everything has been cleaned by the heavy rain, and we sit for a couple of hours chatting, picking, eating, and being thankful that we are able to do this—gathering fruits to make jams for cold, wintry, morning breakfasts by the fire. But those days are still far away. It will be St. John's Day in three weeks, and the days will become lazier and hotter, and we will all feel (or at least I will feel) like we are living in a dream, not altogether present because of the awesome beauty of the gardens, orchards, insects, butterflies, bees, and birds in abundance.

These are beautiful early summer days, with a light breeze blowing over the gardens; it is pleasant to work in the flower beds and do mundane chores. The growth forces are at their height and plants sprout overnight, especially the weeds, which have become enormous. The weeds bring whatever the soil needs, and many of them have a spiky nature and bring light into the soil through the formic acid they contain. How wonderful the Earth's wisdom is; what she lacks, the plant makes and brings to her.

It is late at night and the animals are quiet, except for the howling of coyotes and their young ones looking for something to eat. The young stallion is running around the yard. He will have to be put in a pasture soon, because he destroyed part of my flower bed last night while running free.

A friend came to visit from far away and told me a very funny story that had me in stitches. She told me that her doctor told her to sit in a chamomile bath for one of her complaints. She proceeded to do just that. After running very hot water into a big, metal bowl, she kind of fell into it and got a first-degree burn on her bottom. She was alone at home at the time and called for help. For a few days, she had to sleep on her side and was unable to sit. Meanwhile, the local community priest was applying compresses on her burns. The image was too much for me to resist laughing! I asked, "How could you put yourself in such a predicament?" Life on the farm has its charm.

I made strawberry jam, and the house smelled wonderful. I spent the afternoon chatting with a friend and drinking herbal tea harvested from my garden—Chinese anise sweetened with honey from our bees. They are extremely active now, flying everywhere and gathering nectar. You can see them sitting on the flowers with their tiny legs full, covered in yellow pollen to be carried back to their homes down by the barn. The peonies are almost past their prime and other flowers are coming in. The chickens are scratching away in my new beds and making a mess.

It seems that summer has arrived. We have very warm nights that require a fan for sleeping, as we are serenaded by frogs in the pond and the yelps of coyotes. We are blessed with sunny days that warm the gardens. However, the mornings become too warm around ten o'clock, so I do my farm chores and gardening early. After breakfast, I paint through the day, with a few breaks for writing and reading and then I cook supper, followed by more reading.

Yesterday the two mares got into a skirmish and broke through the partition in the barn. They found themselves in the big meadow, which is not fenced, and had a nice time with the stallion, galloping around the thirty-acre pasture. I had to run to the main gate to close it so that they would not go into the road. I let them run until my husband came home to take care of them and fix the barn.

The farmers have all cut their hay fields now, and everything is nice and neat. The corn and soybean fields are growing rapidly, and summer flowers will make their appearance in another week or so. I saw only one monarch butterfly, but they should be arriving shortly to dance around my flower and herb gardens.

The birds are getting very rowdy in the gardens, singing through the days, from the very early morning until far into the night. The doves eat small ants on the path into the house and do not even bother getting out of the way as I pass. The hummingbird swings back and forth in its dance. Yellow finches flutter about, looking like flying flowers, and the red-winged blackbird becomes very disturbed as I stroll around my garden. He seems to think I am coming for his eggs, which are hidden in the bushes. I always wear a hat, because he often flies straight toward my head to scare me away. The swallows fly acrobatically, low over the pond. They do not sit on rocks and sip water, but touch the surface and drink while flying. As usual, the eagles fly in circles, looking for a snack—my little chicks!

I brought lunch to a friend because I had cooked too much, and we talked late into the afternoon. One very young member of our community, a mother of small children, is facing death. We do our best to help, and we share these words:

> You can't just will or pray pain away.
> You must recognize it for what it is: it's a message.
> A painless existence means a neutral, lightless
>   existence.
> So do not will someone else's pain away.
> With each pain comes a promise of light.
> Pain can crack one open.
> Imagine rocks being cracked,
> cracked that light may enter,
> Imagine jewels being found
> within these rocks.
>
> Pain in itself is never the problem.
> Stubbornness, greed, blindness,
> they are the problems.
> Give thanks for pain
> that it may work into, through, and out of (a soul)
> rightly and quickly.[10]

10. Claire Blatchford, *Friend of My Heart: Meeting Christ in Everyday Life* (Great Barrington, MA: Lindisfarne Books, 1999), p. 101.

Give thank, deep thanks,
for the infirmities,
the afflictions,
the aberrations,
the doubts and fears
of those you love.[11]

Thanks to such words, we grow stronger and face the difficulties of life.

The warmth of the sun is ripening the plants and drying the earth. It is too hot to work in the garden, but today a welcome thunderstorm comes from the southeast and gives relief to the thirsty plants.

Yesterday I spent the afternoon with a friend at a Milwaukee Symphony concert, listening to Mahler's Symphony No. 2, the "Resurrection," directed by German-born Andrea Delft. It brought tears to our eyes at the end, when the Milwaukee Master Chorus chanted the poem based on "Die Auferstehung" (Resurrection) by Friedrich Gottlieb Klopstock:

Rise again, yes, rise again,
Will you, my dust,
After a brief rest!
Immortal life! Immortal life
Will he who called you, give you.

To bloom again were you sown!
The Lord of the harvest goes
And gathers in, like sheaves,
Us together, who died.

---

11. Ibid., p. 104.

O believe, my heart, O believe:
Nothing to you is lost!
Yours is, yes yours, is what you desired
Yours, what you have loved
What you have fought for!

O believe,
You were not born for nothing!
Have not for nothing, lived, suffered!

What was created
Must perish,
What perished, rise again!
Cease from trembling!
Prepare yourself to live!

O Pain, You piercer of all things,
From you, I have been wrested!
O Death, You masterer of all things,
Now, are you conquered!

With wings which I have won for myself,
In love's fierce striving,
I shall soar upward
To the light which no eye has penetrated!
Its wing that I won is expanded,
and I fly up.
Die shall I in order to live.
Rise again, yes, rise again,
Will you, my heart, in an instant!
That for which you suffered,
To God will it lead you!

We were bathed in the encompassing solemnity of the orchestra and the prayerful gestures of the conductor, and as the music ended, our eyes were full of tears. Throughout the concert we were reminded of our friend who is fighting for her life and facing an imminent death while trying to remain alive on earth for her two young daughters. Our whole community is going toward the threshold with her; that is her gift to us. When her daughters asked her if she was going to be with them, she replied that she was trying her hardest: to say such a thing requires immense strength and courage.

❦

My husband has gone again to rejoin my son in the Canadian Rockies to build a winter home. So I am alone for a couple of weeks taking care of the farm. If anything breaks, I am in trouble; if the animals get loose, I am also in trouble. Let's hope all will go well. It seems the bees might be swarming, and again, I can't be of help. They will just fly away, because no one is there to catch them and put them in a new home. My husband and son have daily visitors in their camp: bears! I have requested that they take extra care. I will be up there next winter and fall, but for now it is farm life and a time for agriculture.

As usual, after the storm it is pleasantly cooler, and the horses are quite happy; the flies do not bother them as much. This year we have a new insect here: the cicada. Someone said that this particular species has emerged after seventeen years underground. I saw one yesterday; she had orange eyes, with some orange on her wings and a brown and black body. A friend who came by for eggs said that these cicadas emerge in great numbers to protect the species because they are very tasty to numerous predators. Their wings make an amusing and distinct sound; you would think it was a motor.

The horizon has become dark indigo again. I have to stay off the computer, as a lightening strike could destroy it. Soon, however, the weather settles and becomes cool. Around St. John's Day, it was cool, with a beautiful sunset of warm colors caused by humidity in the air. That morning, the sunrise began to show its aura around four o'clock and lasted quite long, with beautiful light of shimmering yellow becoming green, soft lilac, and then blue purple. Because the sun rises at its most northern point, I could see it all from my bedroom window without getting up; a welcoming sight for such an important date, one of my favorite days.

At the time of the solstice, I feel an urge to erect large stones in the corner of the garden. If I sit in the center of the garden where I have the large statue of Diana inside a round fountain and look into the eastern skies toward the northeastern side of the garden, I see where I would put the stones. On the morning of June 21, it would indicate the point where the sun rises, and one could see the sun come up right above that stone. Actually, I have not put any stones there, because they are too heavy for me, so I have planted a tree there instead. I can see it from my garden. With a natural calendar there would be no need to have the day written down. I would be able to see it from the stones, which I scatter around this circular garden, just like the Druid priests did in ancient times with the stone circles in England, France, and elsewhere.

We have bought a Bobcat tractor, so now we can actually put the stones in that spot in the garden. This will be a

A statue of Diana inside a round fountain

late fall project, one that everyone who owns a farm should design. It takes only a year to plan, and it is wonderful to live with the planets, the sun, the moon, and beautiful, large granite stones. Our friends from long, long ago help us keep time in the sacred spaces.

The spring mood has gone from the garden, and early summer colors are setting in. The bright orange lilies are showing their lovely faces on tall stems that bend gently in the breeze and courageously face the strong tornado-like wind. The black-eyed Susans are coming up slowly. My tiger lilies are being attacked viciously by a rabbit, who loves to cut them and eat the tender yellow-green blossoms. I planted lots of them last year, because they are sturdy and survive our cold winters. They looked so promising, but now I only have a few left. If I could shoot, I would have taken the gun and shot him and cooked him in a wonderful wine stew, a recipe from my grandmother. We had that meal a few weeks ago, made from rabbits that my husband shot in the vegetable garden. They tasted delicious. The recipe is made with tomato sauce and a little curry sauce. The rabbit is cooked gently in olive oil until fried a bit, then covered in the sauce until it is cooked. One may add a bit of red wine, and then cook up some polenta, served with rabbit stew on top.

The chickens are destroying my Spanish moss roses, which I love and are difficult to maintain. They go into the garden when it is dry and take their afternoon bath in the dust. One can hear the daddy rooster calling his ladies: "Hey girls, come over here; the bath is great. It's lovely in the sun and we can bathe in the garden, flap our wings, and let the dust drive away all the insects that bother us. Come." And there go my lovely moss roses, flying in the air, not knowing what hit them. They were lovely in their bright colors, welcoming people to the farm. I can't shoot the chickens, and I can't keep them cooped up. I just have to be vigilant and make sure they stay out of the garden.

The horses escaped again, and this time I did not have my husband to chase after them. Thank goodness I had locked the main door. The two mares were happy, and the young stallion was running around. Then it got hot and they wanted to go back into the barn. However, they were unable to get in and became frustrated. Silky, the older mare, took the lead. But she, too, was unable to find a way into the barn, so they continued to run around until I spoke to them in a gentle voice, telling them that all was fine—to just go back in. Once they were on the opposite side of the big meadow, I opened their main gate and waited until they went back in. They were happy to be in their familiar home. With things back to normal, I left the young stallion with them. That day, I was not in the mood to do much painting, and to make matters worse, the horses had run through my perennial garden, right over my lovely delicate tiger lilies, the ones that the rabbit had been eating.

By late afternoon, the day returned more or less to normal. Then I began to worry about the cows, which I had not seen for days. But very early this morning, I saw them with the sheep, all gathered on the far southern side of the property, eating their breakfast before the heat of the day when the insects would be too much for them. Later, people called and wanted to visit the gallery, and that meant spending the rest of the day cleaning the gallery, my studio, and the house. That night, after all the cleaning, I relaxed with a couple of movies, which doesn't happen often.

Gardening slows down after St. John's Day, and anything not planted will have to wait until next year. But I still have to shovel many wheelbarrows full of manure on top of the flower bed; without the manure, the flowers do not grow. Here are a few words about manure. As the old master of meditation, scientist, and teacher, Georg Kühlewind, used to say when he was about to impart something very important that was meant to shake your inner core, "Hold on to your seats! Get ready for take off! What I am about to say is not for the fainthearted. Get ready."

You have an analogy in Nature when you carry manure to the fields and beautiful plants spring from it. There you have an analogy in Nature except that the dung, the manure, is also perceptible to the senses. So it is when the half-reality of the world of beauty is observed clairvoyantly. Try to envisage this half-real world of beauty, quite apart from the teeming life in the three kingdoms of Nature on the Earth; picture all the beautiful after-effects springing from the Earth. Just as lovely flowers spring up in a meadow, you must spiritually picture underneath it all the Moondung which contains the ugly spidery creatures I have described.[12] Just as cabbage does not grow unless it is manured, as little can beauty blossom on the Earth unless the Gods manure the Earth with ugliness. That is the inner necessity of life. And this inner necessity of life must be known to us, for such knowledge alone can give us the power to confront with understanding what actually surrounds us in Nature.

Anyone who believes that beauty in art can be produced on Earth without the foundation of this ugliness is like a man who is horrified that people use manure, insisting that it would be far better to let beautiful things grow without it. In point of fact it is not possible for beauty to be produced without the foundation of ugliness. And if people do not want to give themselves up to illusion about the world, that is, if they genuinely wish to know the essential and not the illusory, then they must acquire knowledge of these things. Whoever believes that there is art in the world without ugliness does not know what art is. And why not? Simply for the reason that only he who has an inkling of what I have described to you today will enjoy works of art in the right way, for he knows at what cost they are purchased in world-existence. Whoever wants to enjoy works of art

12. He is referring to sylph-like elemental beings of the earthly realm, with which human beings are entangled, leading to the normal human attraction to beauty.

without this consciousness is like a man who would prefer to do away with manure on the fields.[13]

As a painter, these words make me realize the enormous responsibilities of my work. If we can actually truly feel the impact of these words, we can do away with the egotism that often goes with being an artist. As artists, we can picture ourselves as a huge compost heap in which these elemental beings reside, ready to be transformed into beautiful works of art or the enjoyment of art. This is a very different picture from the one most people have of art and artists.

When they are going through a Gallery, people have no inkling ... of how they are strengthened in the interest they take in beautiful pictures by having these hideous spider-like-creatures creeping in and out of their ears and nostrils.

Man's enthusiasm for what is beautiful arises on the foundation of ugliness. That is a cosmic secret, my dear friends. The spur of ugliness is needed in order that the beautiful may be made manifest. And the greatest artists were men who because of their strong bodily constitution, could endure the invasions of these spidery beings in order to produce, let us say, a Sistine Madonna, or the like. Whatever beauty is brought forth in the world has been lifted out of a sea of ugliness through the enthusiasm in the human soul.[14]

13. Rudolf Steiner, *Man and the World of the Stars: The Spiritual Communion of Mankind*, Lecture in Dornach December 16, 1922 (New York: Anthroposophic Press, 1963), pp. 76–77.

14. Ibid., p. 71.

Perhaps this is why I could not do my artistic work anywhere but on a farm. Here I am in daily contact with manure: when I gather the eggs from the chicken coop, when I water the animals and go into the barn, and when I work the soil in the garden, adding heaps of manure. When I enter my studio, from that internalized manure made from elemental beings, I try to create worthy works of art. But I am unable to see or feel these elemental beings, as I clearly have the constitution to withstand them. Reading these lectures gives us the true meaning of humility and perhaps an understanding of why artists never signed their work in ancient times.

Without fail, St. John's wort (*Hypericum perforatum*) always opens its tiny star-like yellow flowers on St. John's Day. I look forward to the magic whereby this plant dutifully awaits the day when the Sun's arch begins to move toward the south again and toward winter. It shows us tiny blossoms and gives us its wonderful healing, yellow-orange oil.

Here is a plant to conjure with, a plant with supernatural powers. The ancient Greeks believed that the fragrance of St. John's wort would cause evil spirits to fly away. The early Christians converted the herb into a symbol of St. John the Baptist because it flowers about the 24th of June, the day the church designated as St. John's Day.[15]

---

15. *Magic and Medicine of Plants: A Practical Guide to Science, History, Folklore, and Everyday Uses of Medicinal Plants* (Pleasantville, NY: Reader's Digest Association, 1986), p. 290.

I did not plant St. John's wort in my garden; it just came one day and has remained ever since. I left room for more plants to come. It is delightful to see the magic that opens on that day after the solstice on June 25. The plant has a definite relationship with the light.

> Although a tea made from the flowers is still used in herbal medicine, some researchers who study herbal teas warn against taking it, because the plant contains hepericin, a photosensitizing substance that reacts with light to cause sunburns in light-skinned persons.[16]

In our area of the country, St. John's wort grows wild along the highways and country roads. It is a very delicate plant, with a lovely strong yellow (yellow cadmium-medium for a painter) five-pointed star like the inside of an apple star. These little flowers produce wonderful oil, which anthroposophic medicine uses for various ailments. I observe St. John's wort on daily rounds of my garden. I try to greet the being of each plant and thank it for its presence in my garden. When we acknowledge these flowers and the beauty they bring us, we release the being that is enchanted in the plant, allowing it to proceed on its own path. Every day I feel the need to visit all the gardens and see who is there waiting to be seen, appreciated, and perhaps picked for a bouquet.

While I was trekking across France in the spring of 2009, I received a nice lavender syrup, which was served to me on a very hot day. My lavender flowers are ready to be picked and I will try to make the syrup, which is a bit complicated, but its light aroma was so enchanting that I must make it and

---

16. Ibid.

St. John's wort flowers in the garden

serve it on hot humid days such as today. I can feel the mood of summer upon us.

> … Now at midsummer, humanity is really enmeshed within the being of nature. From spring onwards into summer, the nature process becomes constantly more active, more inwardly saturated, and human beings become thoroughly interwoven in this nature process. We can indeed say that in high summer human beings experience a kind of nature consciousness. During spring, if they have the perception and feeling for it, they become one with all that is growing and sprouting. They blossom with the flower, germinate with the plant, fruit with the plant, enter into everything that lives and has its being in the world outside. In this way they project

their personality into the being of nature, and a kind of nature-consciousness arises in them....

In summer, human beings are closely enmeshed in nature but, if they have the right feeling and perception for it, objective spirituality comes towards them from nature's interweaving life. And so, to find the essential human being during St John's time, at midsummer we must turn to the objective spirituality in the outer world, and this is present everywhere in nature. Only in outward appearance is nature the sprouting, budding—one might say the sleeping—being which calls forth from the powers of sleep the forces of vegetative growth, in which a kind of sleeping, nature-life is given form. But in this sleeping nature, if only human beings have the perception for it, the spirit that animates and weaves through everything in nature is revealed.

So it is that if at midsummer we follow nature with deepened spiritual insight and with perceptive eyes, we find our gaze directed to the depths of the earth itself. We find that the minerals down there display their inner crystal-forming process more vividly than at any other time of the year. If we look with imaginative perception into the depths of the earth at St John's-tide, we really have the impression that down there are the crystalline forms into which the hard earth consolidates—the very crystalline forms that gain their full beauty at the height of summer. At midsummer everything down below the earth shapes itself into lines, angles and surfaces. If we are to have an impression of it as a whole, we must picture this crystallizing process as an interweaving activity, colored throughout with deep blue.[17]

As I walk in these gardens with all these plants giving their best to us, I often think that we human beings are certainly not giving the best we have, but often the worst. This is why walking and spending time in these enchanted gardens has such a healing effect; they remind us that we have a long way to go if we are to show our best "attire."

And now, for St John's-time, there appears ... an extraordinary earnest countenance. It arises glowing warmly out of the pervading radiant Intelligence....

It is with great earnestness that this representative of the weaving cosmic forces appears in the time of summer, seeking to embody himself in a vesture of light....[18]

... [W]hen we come to the time of sprouting, springing life we can no longer speak of matter permeated by spirit, as we speak of the Earth in winter. We have to speak of spirit woven through with matter.... Then you will come to feel that all this is a kind of background for cosmic, light-filled deeds of [the Archangel] Uriel, and a clear impression of the countenance and gaze of Uriel will appear before you.

---

17. Rudolf Steiner, *The Four Seasons and the Archangels: Experience of the Course of the Year in Four Cosmic Imaginations*, Lecture in Dornach October 12, 1923 (London: Rudolf Steiner Press, 1996), pp. 44–45.

18. Ibid., p. 47.

We feel a deep longing to understand this remarkable gaze, directed downwards, and we have the impression we must look around to find out what it signifies. Its meaning first dawns upon the mind when as human beings we learn to penetrate with spiritual vision still more deeply into the blue, silver-gleaming depths of the earth in summer. And we see that weaving around these silver-gleaming crystalline rays are shapes—disturbing shapes, I might almost call them—which continually gather and dissolve, gather and dissolve.

Then we come to perceive—the vision will be different for everyone—that these shapes are human errors which stand out in contrast to the natural order of regular crystals here below. And it is this contrast that Uriel directs his earnest gaze. Here during the height of summer the imperfections of humankind, in contrast to the regularity of the growing crystal forms, are searchingly scanned. Here it is that from the earnest gaze of Uriel we gain the impression of how the moral is interwoven with the natural world order. Here the moral world order does not exist only in ourselves as abstract impulses. For whereas we habitually look at the realms of nature without asking whether there is morality in the growth of plants, or in the process of crystallization—now we see how at midsummer human errors are woven into the regular crystals which are formed in the normal course of nature.

On the other hand, everything of the nature of human virtue and human excellence rises up with the silver-gleaming lines and is seen as the clouds that envelop Uriel.... It enters into the radiant Intelligence, transmuted into cloud-shaped works of art.[19]

Steiner was able to meet these great imaginations, but we all can find small hints of them. When walking in a garden, I must be quiet, open, and awake, not dreaming. This is difficult when the weather is hot, humid, and scented heavily by wonderful plants. Invariably, I walk out with a kind of sadness, that as human beings we are not paying attention to the message of these great beings who unselfishly give. The other day someone walked into the garden and never stopped talking for the whole walk. She looked at nothing, but just kept talking. I pointed to this plant, and that, and then I gave up. What is the point when someone is blind to all this beauty or unwilling to see it? A physically blind person is better able to feel what is in my garden then most who have physical sight. Jacques Lusseyran, a great French writer who was blind, commented on this. Here I cite him in both French and English:

> *Tell est l'odieuse decouverte: mon espace interieur n'est plus a moi. J'y trouve encore quelques objects personnels, mais comme une epingle dans un tas de foin. Et mon espcace interieur n'est pas non plus aux autres; je n'ai pas eu le projet de le leur donner. Il n'est a personne. Il est jonche d'objects. Il existait deja des cimetieres de voitures, et je m'en plaignais car ils detruisent le paysage. Mais voici qu'a*

---

19. Ibid., pp. 49–50.

mon tour je deviens cimetiere : de mots, de cris, de
musique, de gestes que personne ne fait pour de bon,
d'informations, de recettes, de sequences cent fois
repetees et que personne ne veut.

C'est intendu: toute la soiree j'ai ete distrait. La
television, je ne l'ai pas vraiment regardee. La radio,
elle etait branchee, mais je ne l'ecoutais pas. Quant
a la musique de fond a la cafeteria a midi et dans les
ascenceurs, je ne said meme plus si elle fonctionnait.
Et les reclames, cela fait longtemps que je ne said
plus ce qu'elles dissent. Alors comment pourrais-
je etre attaint? Le piege est la, mais je suis hors du
piege. Du moins, je le crois.

Pourtant, tous ces bruits, tous ces flashs dans ma
tete, il n'y a pas de doute: ils ne sont pas a moi. Mon
moi peut les ignorer, il peut chercher encore a vivre
sans eux. Mais ou vivra-t-il? La place est prise. Le
monde exterieur a seme detritus partout.

Et c'est ici qu'il faut avoir du courage. Le courage
de dire ce qu'au fond nous savons tous, mais ce
don't nous n'avons plus la force de temoigner. Un
etre humain auquel je laisse le droit de me parler
sans etre a mesure de lui repondre n'est pas un etre
humain tout a fait. Ce n'est pas un etre humain,
mais il agit sur moi. Une musique que je n'ai pas
choisi d'ecouter construit in moi des formes. Elle
le fait, meme si je n'ai pas su que je l'entendais. Et
ces formes ne sont plus de la musique; elle galopent
sans ordre, elles me modelent a mon insu. /./

Il n'y aura bientot plus un pouce de notre espace interieur qui ne soit pietine chaque jour. L'amour, l'amour lui meme deviant spectacle: on s'est mis a le faire devant nous.

Tout cela ne serait pas tres grave si les hommes n'etaient que des machines. Mais il se trouve qu'ils sont un peu autre chose, car ils possedent un moi. Et le moi a ses regles. Employons un autre mot: le moi a ses conditions de croissance. Il se nourrit uniquement des mouvements qu'il fait. Ceux que d'autres font a sa place, loin de l'aider, l'appauvrissent.[20]

Such is the terrible discovery: my inner space is no longer mine. I can still find a few personal objects like a needle in a hay stack. And to make matter worse, my own personal space does not belong to others either; it was not mine to give. It does not belong to anyone. It is full of stuff. There used to be a cemetery for cars and I used to complain about them because they destroyed the beauty of the country side. But now, it is my turn to become a cemetery: cemetery made of dead words, screams, music, meaningless gestures, information, facts, recipes, and habits a thousand times repeated with no interested witnesses.

It is true: during the whole evening I was distracted. The television, I did not really look at it. The radio, it was on, but I was not listening. As for the back-

---

20. Jacques Lusseyran, *Contre la Pollution du Moi* (Paris: Triades-Solear, 1992), pp. 19–21.

ground music in the cafeteria during lunch time, or in the elevator, I do not even know if it was on. And what about the advertisements, it has been a long time since I have paid attention to them. So how could that stuff ever reach me? The trap is there, but I am outside of that trap. At least that is what I think.

Nevertheless, all this background stuff, which exists in my head, without a doubt it does not belong to me; My own self, or ego can ignore them, can try to live in the center of this chaos without it. But where is this self going to live? The outside world has sown, planted its garbage everywhere within my self.

And that is where we require enormous courage. The courage to say what we all know but dare not say, or witness. A human being whom I allow to speak to me without being able to answer it back, is no longer a real human being. It is no longer a human being, but it has power over myself. Music which I chose to listen to, builds itself certain forms within my psyche. It does this even though I did not consciously hear it. And all these forms within me, are no longer music, they gallop within my psyche, without order, they mold my psyche without my own awareness.

Soon there will no longer be one inch of our own inner space which is not trampled everyday by these forms. Even love, the great Love itself is becoming a spectacle: people are doing it in front of us.

All of this would not be so serious if human beings were only machines. But it happens to be that human beings are a little more. They happen to have an Ego. And this ego has its own laws. Let us use another word: our Ego has its own laws according to which it lives, and grows. It nourishes itself according to what is given to it, according to the movements it assumes. The movements which are done in its place, far from help the Ego, make it much poorer.[21]

This makes it clear why some cannot see the beauty in front of them and the source of that blindness. Living on a farm is one of the fastest ways to regain our inner space and fill it with meaningful form beings, strengthening our "I," space, and mind.

❧

I sat in the garden and took a coffee break while the chickens came looking for something to eat. The rooster stood proudly, looking over his dominion and keeping the hens in order. Two tiny hummingbirds flew within an inch of my ear, chasing each other. Meanwhile, the little rabbit was running around and eating my plants, cute I admit, with his little white tail.

Weeds! Weeds! Weeds! They are glorious weeds and growing taller than I am. Now I have to get into the vegetable garden, which I have completely ignored. The tomato plants seem lost among these weeds, so I have to get to work,

21. Jacques Lusseyran, *Against the Pollution of the I: Selected Writings of Jacques Lusseyran* (Sandpoint, ID: Morning Light Press, 2006), pp. 19–21.

even though it's getting into the heat of the day. It's late morning, and the temperature is reaching the nineties—too hot for me. I manage to finish one area, and tomorrow I will return around seven o'clock, right after taking care of the chickens. Back at the house, my face is beet-red and I am perspiring as if I had run a marathon. Perhaps I'm getting too old for this.

> In a little corner of the garden, the stinging nettles have reserved a little patch for themselves. I let them grow there, as they are an important part of the garden "weeds." Basically, I let them grow wherever they wish. The stinging nettle has at least three properties that illustrate its dynamic character: 1) it helps neighboring plants grow more resistant to spoilage; 2) it changes the chemical process in companion crops—for example, the content of essential oils increase up to twenty percent in valerian and ten percent in sage and peppermint; 3) it stimulates humus formation.

> The stinging nettle has fine hairs on its leaves and stems and contains formic acid and perhaps a poison. Nettles were known to the ancients for their medicinal value, thought to increase blood circulation and used as a stimulant. Moreover, very young plants can be cooked like spinach during early spring as an excellent edible green, rich in vitamins and iron. Nettles were also used traditionally as a remedy for anemia and to increase vitality.[22]

22. Helen Philbrick and Richard Gregg, *Companion Plants and How to Use Them* (Kimberton, PA: Biodynamic Farming and Gardening Association, 2008), p. 84.

Nettles show strength and uprightness and perfection of form. Their form, particularly that of the stings, is shaped by silica. The strength of the sting is an important indication of the value of the nettle in making the biodynamic Preparation 504.

According to Steiner, the nettle is a plant with unique healing qualities for both humans and plants. If you sketch the nettle plant and draw a line to connect up the nodal points or axils of each leaf, you find the double spiral form of the spiritual staff of Mercury— the medical sign.

The forces of Mars that influence the nettles bring iron, magnesium and other minerals, such as sulphur. These forces also have an iron-regulating effect....[23]

Stinging nettle works like magic in the garden. Through its silica content, it brings light into the clayish soil of my garden. Other spiky weeds also bring great silica light into the garden. They balance soil that lacks sufficient light. For more on this subject, see Nicolaus Remer's *Laws of Life in Agriculture*.[24]

23. Peter Proctor with Gillian Cole, *Grasp the Nettle: Making Biodynamic Farming and Gardening Work* (New Zealand: Random House, 2004), pp. 73–74.

24. Nicolaus Remer, *Laws of Life in Agriculture* (Wyoming, RI: Biodynamic Literature, 1995).

The rabbit had come for his breakfast and destroyed more of my beautiful tiger lilies. This time he chewed the thick stem. Perhaps I will give him some carrots at the beginning of the path and then he can leave my garden alone, or grow some stuff just for him. I am being nice to him, but this weekend he will be gone. A hunter is coming!

I watered the cows, sheep, and horses and noticed that the honeybees were very active. Their beehives are by the little barn, and they were flying fast. Most of the time I simply forget they are there and doing their wonderful job, except when I see them in my garden, and today I left them water in a shallow container.

I walked the fence to see if any trees had fallen on it. We seldom visit the large meadows in the back. The cows, horses, and sheep do that. The thirty acres are full of ancient oak and hickory trees. It is part of the large oak savannah that covers much of Wisconsin, extending to Minnesota. This land on the western side of the property has a quiet, gentle strength. I am sure many elementals live there undisturbed. It is pleasant to have an area left undisturbed where these beings can reside. When I walk there, I walk softly, quietly, to avoid interfering with them. In contrast to my flower and herb gardens, where the elementals enjoy visitors, this area likes to remain wild, visited only by their friends the coyotes, foxes, birds, and other creatures. The oaks, the Druid trees, are the kings there.

Oak: the Oak is hospitable to and aids other trees....

Biodynamic preparation number 505 is made from red- or white-oak bark from not too old a tree, treated in a special way.

The oak tree has the special property of accumulating a tremendous amount of calcium in its bark during growth. In fact, the highest calcium ash content was found in oak trees growing on a sandy calcium-deficient soil. The calcium content of this bio-dynamic prep is therefore very high. This preparation in its effect stimulates the resistance of plants to disease.[25]

I recall the first time I made this preparation. It was during our second year on the farm, and we'd had one of our two-year-old bulls butchered. I picked up the head at the butcher and brought it home. I followed the procedure and cleaned it out with a friend. We sat way in the back of the property, because I thought it might be awkward if the post lady were to come with our mail and see us sitting there with a huge bull head on our laps, full of blood and trying to clean it up, and inserting the ground oak from a tree at the back of the land. How would I explain such an activity? We had a good laugh at our new activities on the farm.

I found the wet spring toward the back of our land and buried the head, where it would stay for the winter. However, several days later, the dog had dug it up, so I buried it again. This time it remained in the ground until I dug it out, removed the oak bark, and put it in the basement.

---

25. Philbrick and Gregg, *Companion Plants and How to Use Them*, p. 65.

During summer, I like to take pictures of the garden. I treasure the little photo paintings as reminders that all the hard work was worth it—the sweat and aches of the heavy spring gardening.

This afternoon, it is time to go for a swim in our "Piss Pond," as I call it. Our town has a small lake, or pond, a remnant of the receding glacier many hundreds of thousands of years ago. The people in town, as well as people from a neighboring town, all bring their kids to the pond, hence the nickname. I usually go for a swim around five or six o'clock in the evening, after everyone has gone home. It is quiet and I can enjoy the murky colored waters and the muddy bottom after sweating all day. I dislike air-conditioning, and I leave my house at least fifty times a day, so it doesn't make sense to have it anyway. It also seems very unhealthy for my body to keep switching from cool to hot; it may be better to let the body take care of itself. We have large ceiling fans instead, which work quite well.

This time of the year I sincerely miss the glorious New Hampshire granite, crystal-clear mountain lakes where I swam for so many years when my children were growing up. Now I have the "Piss Pond," and I have actually grown a bit fond of it.

The colors are becoming magnificent in the garden, so I especially enjoy my walks there. Some plants seed themselves and I have combinations which I would never expect—bright orange with light pink! And this year the black-eyed Susans are mixed with the deep purple-magenta, peach, and pink spires of the hollyhocks. The garden is one wonder

Black-eyed Susans and hollyhocks in the garden

after another. My dog seems to enjoy it as well, especially digging for little underground animals.

When we observe a flower with the eye of the spirit we cannot help but experience it to be like our own soul when it cherishes the tenderest desires. Only look at a spring flower; it is a breath of longing, the embodiment of a wish. And something wonderful streams forth over the world of flowers that surrounds us, if only our soul perception is delicate enough to be open to it.

In spring, we see the violet, maybe the daffodil, the lily-of-the-valley, or some plants with yellow flowers, and we are seized by the feeling that these spring-flowering plants would say to us: O, man, how pure and innocent can be the desires which you direct toward the spiritual! Spiritual desire nature, desire nature bathed, as it were in godliness, breathes from every spring flower.

And when the later flowers appear—let us go straight to the other extreme, let us take the autumn crocus— can one behold the autumn crocus with soul perception without having a slight feeling of shame? Does it not warn us that our desires can become impure, that our desires can be imbued with every kind of corruption? It is as though the autumn crocuses spoke to us from all sides, as if they would continually whisper to us: Consider the world of your desires, O, man; how easily you can become a sinner!

Looked at thus, the plant world is the mirror of human conscience in external nature. Nothing more poetical can be imagined than the thought of this voice of conscience, which in us comes forth as though from a single point, distributed over the many different kinds of flowers that speak to the soul during the seasons of the year in the most manifold ways. The plant world reveals itself as the outspread mirror of conscience if we know how to look at it aright.[26]

---

26. Steiner, *Harmony of the Creative Word*, pp. 188–189.

... [I]n the flowers of the plant kingdom we see, as it were, human conscience laid out before us. What we see outside us may be considered as the picture of our inner life.[27]

Fourth of July weekend and the gardens are reaching their peak, as are the weeds. Horses and sheep escaped again, because my husband left the gate open. We drove the sheep back in and will deal with the horses later. The corn and soybeans are growing fast in the fields for miles and miles around. The lilies are flowering bright orange, yellow, and all shades in between, as well as the tiger lilies—whatever is left of them—which are all very dignified with their tall stems.

The lily has always been regarded as the symbol of purity and is one of the oldest flowers in the world. It may be found painted on the walls of ancient Greek palaces where it was the personal flower of Hera, the Moon Goddess.

The lily is dedicated to the Virgin Mary in honor of her purity which is perhaps why so many brides like to include it in their bouquets and why it may be found at many religious festivals. Legend has it that the first lily sprang up from the tears dropped by Eve when she left the Garden of Eden.[28]

How then does the visible part of the plant really come into being? If you have the physical body, for instance, a quartz crystal, you can see the physical

27. Ibid., p. 212.

28. Sheila Pickles, *The Language of Flowers: Penhaligon's Scented Treasury of Verse and Prose* (New York: Harmony Books, 1990).

in an unmediated way. But with a plant you do not really see the physical, you see the etheric form. This etheric form is filled out with physical matter; physical substances live within it. When the plant loses its life and becomes carbon in the earth you see how the substance of physical carbon remains....

Thus, the physical becomes visible for us in the mineral world. In the world of the plants the physical has already become invisible, for what we see is really the etheric made visible through the agency of the physical. We would not, of course, see the plants with our ordinary eyes if the invisible etheric body did not carry within it little granules (an oversimplified and crude expression, to be sure) of physical matter. Through the physical the etheric form becomes visible to us; but this etheric form is what we are really seeing. The physical is, so to speak, only the means whereby we see the etheric. So that the etheric form of a plant is an example of an Imagination, but of an Imagination that is not directly visible in the spiritual world but only becomes visible through physical substances.

If you were to ask, "what is an Imagination?"—We could answer that the plants are all Imaginations, but as Imaginations they are visible only to imaginative consciousness. That they are also visible to the physical eye is due to the fact that they are filled with physical particles whereby the etheric is rendered visible in a physical way to the physical eyes. But if we want to speak correctly we should never say that in the plant we are seeing something physical. In the plants we are seeing genuine Imaginations.

We have imaginations all around us in the forms of the plant world.[29]

Among the hundreds of flowers growing in the garden right now, some of them are mentioned in my little book:

Bluebell *constancy*
Carnation *alas my poor heart*
Columbine *folly*
Cornflower *delicacy*
Daisy *innocence*
Dandelion *oracle*
Forget-me-not *true love*
Geranium *melancholy*
Hollyhock *female ambition*
Iris *message*
Lavender *distrust*
Nasturtiums *patriotism*
Pansy *thoughts*
Peony *shame and bashfulness*
Phlox *agreement*
Poppy *fantastic extravagance*
Primrose *early youth*
Rose *love*
Speedwell *female fidelity*
Tulip *declaration of love*
Violet *modesty*
Wallflower *fidelity in adversity*
Water lily [in my little pond] *purity of heart*[30]

29. Rudolf Steiner, *The Mystery of the Trinity and the Mission of the Spirit*, Lecture in Dornach July 28, 1922 (Hudson, NY: Anthroposophic Press, 1991), pp. 31–32.

30. Pickles, *The Language of Flowers*, pp. 8–9.

And it is a nice exercise to try and see what we come up with as we look at all the different plants. Perhaps we agree with these listed above.

Wisconsin people do not have a French *Cote d'Azur* or a Spanish *Costa del Sol*, but we have the *cote des cherries*. Up north, in Door County, people go to get relief from the heat of the prairies and farms. Cherry trees are abundant in this arm of land reaching out into the great Lake Michigan. We were there a few years ago, by a little island on the lake. It happened to be very warm that year, and it was like being in Hawaii, with its beautiful sandy beach, lovely trees, crystal-clear water, and lovely swimming. People flock there to enjoy the water and the cherry trees.

About 30 minutes from our farm is a very large orchard where we can pick sour cherries, and it is a pleasure to go there the first week in July when all the trees begin ripening. On a weekend many cars arrive there, mostly from Chicago. People are picnicking everywhere, speaking unfamiliar languages. Since I speak Persian, I could understand some of them and I knew many were from the Middle East, from Afghanistan or Iran, there to have picnics and pick cherries. Sour cherries are part of the Middle Eastern diet, and cherry picking is a festive summer activity, one which I enjoyed when I lived in Iran. We would go to my father-in-law's large garden outside of Tehran for the weekend and pick fruits.

Here in the middle of Wisconsin, I think for a moment that I am back in the Middle East with everyone picking— aunts, grandmas, babies, toddlers, the whole family and extended family picking fruit and having a good time. They bring their *chelo-kabab*, and all the paraphernalia for eating outside, even the rice cooker. It must evoke memories of better times in their own countries.

❧

More running around after the horses; I got two of them back, but the older mare Silky would not go in, as she is stubborn. So I left her outside. I ran after the sheep and they obediently went right back in. These horses are truly magnificent creatures, but overwhelming, and they can truly read our thoughts and feelings. I find they are too big for me to feel totally comfortable with them. A few years ago, however, I witnessed my friend's daughter, who was around 11 years old, become a wonderful, courageous, strong *cavaliere*. I would not have thought that she would become a very strong rider. She was a tiny child, meek, skinny, and quite ordinary, except for her lively intelligent eyes. But when I saw her riding several years later, atop an enormous 17-hand, hot-blooded thoroughbred, she had become someone else. She was completely in control, sure of herself, tall and majestic. That horse and rider were a team. She jumped over obstacles, using all sorts of maneuvers. Although she was still thin and small, she made him do whatever she wanted. It was a wonder to see the love between the great, powerful animal and the lovely, determined young girl with absolutely no fear, only trust between animal and human being.

Horses are quite a mystery to me, but I do not give up and must deal with my fears.

> ... The etheric lives in the form of the plant. But in animals we must recognize the existence of something that is not driven to the surface.... The animal moves about freely. There is something in the animal that does not come to the surface and become visible. This is the astral in the animal, something

The horses: a young stallion, two mares, and an Arab gelding

which cannot be grasped by merely making our ideas mobile.... This does not suffice for the astral. If we want to understand the astral we must go further and say that something enters into the etheric and is then able, from within outward, to enlarge the form—for example, to make the form nodular or tuberous. In the plant you must always look outside for the cause of the variation in form, for the reasons why the form changes. You must be flexible with your idea. But the merely mobile is not enough to comprehend the animal. To comprehend the animal you have to bring something else into your concepts. If you want to understand how the conceptual activity appropriate for understanding animals must differ from that for plants, then you need more than a mobile concept capable of assuming different forms ...

That infusion of life is what makes a merely imagined concept into an inspired concept. When it is a plant that is concerned, you can picture yourself inwardly at rest and merely changing the concepts. But if you want to think a true concept of an animal (most people do not like to do this at all because the concept must become inwardly alive; it wriggles within) then you must take the Inspiration, the inner liveliness, into yourself, it is not enough to externally weave sense perceptions from form to form. You cannot think an animal in its totality without taking this inner liveliness into the concept.

... [W]ith the animal we have to bring in Inspiration, and only through Inspiration can we penetrate to the astral....

With an animal we must say that what we see is really not the physical but a physically appearing Inspiration. This is the reason why, when the inspiration or breathing of a person is disturbed in some way it very easily assumes an animal form. Try sometime to remember some of the figures that appear in nightmares. Very many of them appear in animal forms. Animals forms are forms filled with Inspirations.[31]

---

31. Steiner, *The Mystery of the Trinity and the Mission of the Spirit*, Lecture in Dornach July 28, 1922, pp. 33–35.

❧

Again it is Saturday and I pick up fresh whole milk and let it sit in the refrigerator. Then I take the cream from the top, put it in the blender at medium-slow speed, and go about my business. Some 10 minutes or so later, the cream has gone from whipped cream to butter. I put all through a cheese cloth—courtesy of my husband's hospital operating room; they throw everything out, including these great cloths— squeeze the liquid out, and put the remaining butter in the refrigerator. The liquid part goes back into the milk or to the dog for a snack. When the butter hardens 30 minutes later, it is put in a plastic bag and into the freezer, or I mix some fresh thyme into it. The rest waits until I get the urge to make pastries. These past two weeks, I made lots of little tarts filled with custard, topped with fresh strawberries. One cannot live on a farm without giving recipes, so here is the recipe for the tarts:

> Fill a container with about 2 cups of organic whole wheat flour.
>
> Add a mixture of ⅓ butter, ⅓ oil, and ⅓ water to equal one cup or so. Add some sugar.
>
> Mix everything, adding more flour or water to make the mixture workable, but don't work it too much.
>
> Use your fingers to line small tart containers or one pie plate with the mixture.
>
> Bake in a 375-degree oven for 14-16 minutes or more, until golden.
>
> Cool the crust and add a custard mixture and fresh fruit. It is delicious!

'The promised land, where milk and honey flow' has been the timeless yearning of the human race. But it is based on a true vision of wholesome living which might deserve the title 'human'. We would like to get to the bottom of this mystery.

Milk, as we have seen, is mankind's original and oldest food. It was manna from heaven at the time when earth's atmosphere ... was permeated with a milk-like protein substance, the last remnant of which is our present-day nitrogen. This was the beginning of man's earthly evolution. He started using the milk of his animals from the very beginning, and has continued to do so ever since. We see this period of evolution repeated in each individual's infancy and childhood.

Milk prepares the body for habitation by the soul and spirit. It brings a person down to earth and gives him a feeling for the oneness of the human race. Everyone among us breathes air that we own in common with our fellow men. Perhaps, buried deep within us, there is at work the memory of having partaken in common of a cosmic milk, that still gives us a sense of social bond between man and man. Rudolf Steiner tells us that in fact milk prepares man for being a creation of the earth, without preventing him from being a citizen both of the earth and of the whole solar system. To go without milk would estrange us from the earth and make us lose all connection with and feeling for man's earthly task. Therefore, says Rudolf Steiner, we do well, even as adults, to let ourselves be gently tied down here by taking milk.

So we find milk to be a help in incarnating ourselves properly and thus a suitable food during the first half of our lives.[32]

Tomorrow is vinegar day. I have some great estragon (tarragon) plants in the garden which I love to eat for breakfast with cheese and bread. I have a dozen quarts of good organic cider vinegar and I will add as much estragon as I can manage to stuff inside these bottles. Then I will put the tops back on and leave them on the southern side of the farmhouse on the porch in the direct sunlight for the rest of the summer. The vinegar acquires the taste of the estragon and is a nice addition to vinaigrette, perhaps as a gift to a friend. In September it goes into the cellar awaiting further use. It is also an excellent remedy for the intestines.

It is evening here, and quiet on the farm except for the noise of the neighbors who have relatives visiting to celebrate the rites of the Fourth of July. Everyone on a farm here has fireworks, so I go up on the roof and watch the displays from the surrounding farms. The major display was cancelled because of thunderstorms, lightening, and rain. My husband, who is on-call, treats the casualties at the hospital. It is a very busy weekend there between motorcycle accidents, fireworks mishaps, and babies born. We have noticed here that sometimes the baby hospital is very busy at certain times in the summer and invariably, exactly 280 days earlier it had been a snowy, cold weekend. One needs to keep warm!

Before retiring, I go to the vegetable garden and pick fresh mint to make some strong Moroccan green tea to have now, and to place some of it out to dry for winter use.

---

32. Rudolf Hauschka, *Nutrition: A Holistic Approach* (East Sussex: Sophia Books/Rudolf Steiner Press, 2002), p. 83.

The gardens look fantastic—the monarch butterflies are showing up, and the birds are singing from morning until night. I am still trying to cut some of the Great Burdock. It is an extremely tenacious plant, with great vitality and, as a trained herbalist, I should be drying the root for remedies, but I can't do it. I spent an hour cutting them down before they invaded the entire property.

> The pesky burs adorn large-leaved plants whose roots, seeds, leaves, and flowers have long been used for both medicine and food. In the Middle Ages great burdock leaves were pounded with wine to create a remedy for leprosy. The roots were considered effective in allaying high fevers, gout and skin problems. Centuries later the Pennsylvania Dutch brewed a tea from the year-old root to use as a tonic....
>
> Young burdock leaves may be used as salad greens and flavorings for soups. The young roots and stem can be eaten after being boiled twice, with a change of water after the first boiling.[33]

I always leave one huge plant so I can observe it. Burdock root is one of the best remedies, useful for kidney problems, and it has great cleansing properties. Our gardens are full of wonderful weeds. We just have to wean ourselves from easy pharmaceutical solutions and go back to simpler lifestyles. I decide to pick a few of the great roots after all and dry them for future use.

The other weed is Star Thistle, which grows everywhere. The birds, especially the yellow-black-white finches, love the seeds, but they make walking difficult and painful.

---

33. *Magic and Medicine of Plants*, p. 201.

> Despite its prickly nature, star thistle has a number of virtues. The young scales of the flower head are edible like an artichoke, and in parts of North Africa the young, tender stem and leaves complement the salads.[34]

These two abundant weeds on the farm come to balance the earth by bringing in light, in the form of silica, into the dirt. Since we have been on the farm for almost 10 years now, we have lots of worms, showing healthy activity in the soil.

Now it is time for currant picking, and making all sorts of jellies, jams, and syrup. The elderberry flowers, from which I usually make a syrup, are almost finished. The syrup tastes refreshing during the summer, but I missed harvesting some this year, although I still have some left from past years. The peaches are slowly ripening, but it will not be a great year for them, since only three or four of the trees have fruit. The pear trees are taking a rest this year, but the apples look abundant and so do the plums. Plum jam is one of my favorites, probably because it reminds me of my Italian grandmother's jams, all lined up neatly in her large basement in Dijon.

In the flower garden, the lilies are starting to open and show us their beauty. I have planted them everywhere, as they are quite hardy and give us a show in the first weeks of July. They take over after the irises have gone. They are plants which I call showy and selfish; their gesture is one of self-sufficiency. They grow out of common thick root systems but are beyond the onion-bulb type of plant, such as the spring plants, like tulips, which are even more selfish. They do not need the environment; they live off their

---

34. Ibid., p. 308.

own bulb. The other plants which grow during August or the end of July are more social plants. They have better-developed root systems underground. With multiple bulbs, their gesture is more that of a social plant, such as those of the compositae family—daisies, black-eyed Susans, yarrow, or tansy. One learns much from watching these plants, especially observing the times of the summer in which they grow.

Many years ago I took a three-week summer class at the Steiner Institute in Maine with Dennis Klocek, a wonderful teacher, artist, writer, and alchemist (see Docweather.com for a list of his books). I learned much about plants, even though I had studied herbalism for a few years and became a trained herbalist through Dominion College in British Columbia, besides growing my own gardens for many years. What Dennis had to teach was beyond my expectations, and anyone seriously interested in plants should attend one of his workshops or a few months at Rudolf Steiner College in Sacramento, California, where he teaches. Since studying with Dennis, I look at plants and see what influences are coming from the cosmos, or from the earth, simply by looking at the plants. They begin to tell their stories if we know what to look for. Is it a central force in the plant, coming from the center outward, or is it a centrifugal force coming from the outside toward the center? One can examine all the plants and see what is present, thereby determining the forces which are active. So we see if it is a more cosmic plant with influence coming from the outside, or a more earthly plant with influence coming from the inside.

Here is a more complex insight into these forces taken from Rudolf Steiner's famous Agriculture course.

We have seen the need to make strict distinctions among the forces active in plant growth. On the one hand, there are forces that actually originate in the cosmos, but which are first absorbed into the Earth and then work on the plants from there. These forces—which as I indicated essentially originate from the cosmic influences of Mercury, Venus and the Moon, but which work in a roundabout way via the Earth rather than directly from the planets— these are the forces we need to take into account when we trace how one generation of plants leads to the next. On the other hand, in everything plants acquire from the periphery, from what is above the Earth, we need to look to the various effects that the distant planets transmit to the air, and which are taken up in that way. Furthermore, we can say that everything coming from the near planets (Venus, Mercury, Moon)—in the way of forces working into the Earth—is heavily influenced by the lime in the Earth, while everything coming from the distant periphery (Mars, Jupiter, Saturn) is influenced by the silica. And even when the silica influences proceed from the Earth itself, they still transmit what comes from Jupiter, Mars, and Saturn, and not what comes from Moon, Mercury, and Venus.

Nowadays we are not in the habit of taking these things into account, but we're also having to pay for it....[35]

---

35. Steiner, *Agriculture*, p. 114.

It is obvious that enormous changes must occur for the human being to become a priest working as a farmer. We are being asked to completely open our minds to the Great Cosmos. A friend of mine jokingly puts it this way: "From strawberries to Jupiter!"

❧

Today it will be around 100 degrees in the heartland, very warm indeed, but there is still a little breeze. I could not go to Sunday morning breakfast at Benta and Walter Goldstein's home because my chores were not finished. I had to make sure the animals had enough water for such a hot day. I regret this because I have enjoyed the gatherings at this well-known home over the last ten years and have met quite a variety of people there. Walter's work in corn breeding has taken him all over the world, and he employs students from Ecuador, Peru, Thailand, Russia, Mexico, and many other places to help him with his research. They invariably are fed and entertained by Benta, Walter's Norwegian wife. At these gatherings, I have met:

an Old Russian Jewish grandma émigré
a young lady doctoral student in physics from India
lovely girls from southern and northern Thailand
Korean ministers
Japanese students
Ecuadorian Indian agriculture experts
Native American chiefs from reservations
local homeschooling ladies
a financial maverick from Chicago
a wealthy old German industrial tycoon

singers
Chicago-Romanian Seventh-day Adventists
Jewish-Dutch troubadours from Chicago
a local veterinarian team traveling between New
    Zealand and the U.S.
activists in local town politics
artists
an agricultural attaché from Moldova
a German agriculturalist
promising cellists and violinists and their three sons
young men and women from Germany who needed
    a place to stay for a month or so
children who are educated at home (by Benta)
teenagers who needed to be straightened out
young housewives learning how to cook and care
    for a family
an unattached single woman who had no home
local anthroposophists
a pharmacist who travels between New Zealand
    and the U.S.
Benta's relatives from Norway who have become
    my relatives
her delightful mother
and many others dropping in at all times of the
    year, day, or season for socializing, including
    me, who needs to engage with warm souls once
    in a while and share a great cup of coffee

People from large cities such as New York or Chicago
think that they are where the action is and that people in the
heartland are unfortunate because they have nothing to do.
Perhaps here we are undertaking a new way to be, with no

regard to color, race, religion, or economic status. Benta was brought up in an anthroposophical household, and in her life she does not need to try to implement these values; they are part of her. She is truly present to visitors. We cannot ask more than this, because to be truly present for someone is to love them. And when one joins Walter on one of his famous corn walks, one can truly see that he loves his plants, and perhaps that is why Native American chiefs come here, to see that perhaps not all is lost.

Neither Walter nor Benta do this for money; their impulse comes from their large, open hearts and lives, and it is not easy for them financially. Walter must spend countless hours on his computer looking for funding for his worthwhile work. It does not come easily.

> ... The old connection between the workman and his work is no longer possible, but man needs a relationship to his work. It is necessary that he should feel joy in his work, that he should feel a certain devotion to it. The old devotion, the immediate companionship with the thing he has made, exists no longer; yet it must be replaced by something else. What can this be? It can only be replaced by enlarging men's horizons, by raising them to a level on which they can come together with their fellow men in one great circle, eventually with all their fellow men within the same social organism as themselves, in which they can develop an interest in man as man. It must come to pass that even the man who is working in the most remote corner at a single screw for some great machine need not put his whole self into the contemplation of the screw, but it must come about

that he can carry into his workshop the feelings that
he entertains for his fellow men, that when he leaves
his workshop he finds the same feelings, that he has
a living insight, into his connection with human
society, that he can work even without actual pleasure in his production because he feels he is a worthy
member in the circle of his fellow men.[36]

... To say that egoism must be overcome by love does
not help us much to understand egoism. For the point
is, that he who meets his fellow men with a purely
human interest and understanding acts differently
from one whose interests are narrow, and who gives
no thought to all that fills the hearts and souls of his
fellow creatures, and who is without interest for his
surroundings. On this account, the former, who is
truly interested in his fellow men, need not be less ego-
istic in life than the other because his egoism may be
precisely his desire to serve human beings. It may call
forth in him a feeling of inner well-being, of inner bliss,
even of ecstasy, to devote himself to the service of his
fellow men. Then, as far as the outer life is concerned,
deeds that are absolutely altruistic to all appearance
may proceed from egoism; in the life of feeling they
cannot be appraised otherwise than as egoism.[37]

... There are two absolutely distinct sources in human
nature from which arise, respectively, nationalism and
internationalism. Nationalism is the highest development of egoism. Internationalism is what permeates

36. Rudolf Steiner, *The Social Future*, Lecture in Zurich October 1919
(NY: Anthroposophic Press, 1972), p. 70.

37. Ibid., p. 130.

us more and more as we give ourselves to a wide understanding of human nature. We must regard the common life of human beings all over the civilized globe in this light, especially if we wish to come to a clear understanding of the conflicting element in these impulses, nationalism and internationalism....[38]

I must say that, if we had to put a flag on our porch or our lawn as all do in this area, we would have to put up several flags. My own yard would look like the United Nations: France, Tunisia, Iran, Bahamas, Canada, and the good old USA, and with the children we would have to add a few more, considering where they travel. In some places that welcome people from all over the world, each day they put up the flag of the visiting guests.

Outside, the birds are singing, and I just fed the fish in the pond. They loved my old blueberry muffins. The horses are trying to keep cool in the barn where the flies do not bother them so much. In the vegetable garden, the tomatoes are slowly ripening. I bought some from a small farm where they grow them indoors. I did not ask if they used pesticides or fertilizers. When it gets hot, there is nothing like a nice juicy tomato sandwich. In another couple of weeks, it will be the beginning of canning season—more work, but enjoyable.

The studio is awaiting me. I have a four-by-five foot Pieta watercolor painting to finish and, besides these anecdotes of farm life, I am working on another manuscript about my last 800 km walk from Le Puy, France to Jaca, Spain this past spring. So life on the farm is anything but boring. Last night a friend who had just flown to her second home in Ecuador, then to Ireland and back here to the Midwest, came by for a

---

38. Ibid., p. 132.

ladies' night out. She is an investment banker and only, she says, deals with families who are worth over a hundred million dollars, and only invests in good-for-everyone ventures. I love to argue with her, because I do not believe in saving money or keeping it. In our family we spend it all—on worthwhile adventures of course—and the rest we give away to those who need it, such as Prison Outreach, Sophia House in California, Homes for Children in Brazil, SteinerBooks, and so on. This we think is better than accumulating funds in the bank and letting the bank do what it wants with it.

❧

The afternoon sun is scorching the fields, but the tall elm trees are giving their gentle shade. The gardens are intoxicating, their heavenly scents making one feel sleepy.

Titania
Come, sit thee down upon this flowery bed,
While I thy amiable cheeks do coy,
And stick musk-roses in thy sleek smooth head,
And kiss thy fair large ears, my gentle joy.

Bottom
Where's Peas-Blossom?

Peas-Blossom
Ready.

Bottom
Scratch my head, Peas-Blossom.—Where's
Monsieur Cobweb?

Cobweb
Ready.

Bottom
Monsieur Cobweb, good monsieur, get your
weapons in your hands and kill me a red-hipt
humble-bee on the top of a thistle; and good
monsieur, bring me the honey-bag. Do not fret
yourself too much in the action, monsieur; and,
good monsieur have a care the honey-bag break
not; I would be loth to have you overflown
with a honey-bag, signior.—Where's Monsieur
Mustard-seed?

Mustard-seed
Ready.

Bottom
Give me your neif, Monsieur Mustard-seed.
Pray you, leave your courtesy, good monsieur.

Mustard-seed
What's your will?

Bottom
Nothing, good monsieur, but to help Cavalry
Peas-Blossom to scratch. I must to the barber's,
monsieur; for methinks I am marvelous hairy about
the face; and I am such a tender ass, if my hair do
but tickle me, I must scratch.[39]

---

39. William Shakespeare, "A Midsummer Night's Dream," Act IV,
Scene 1. In *The Complete Works of William Shakespeare: Gathered
into One Volume* (NY: Oxford University Press, n.d.), p. 294.

I could not resist William's lines after a walk in the garden. My own words are inadequate.

"Cocorico!" in French; "Cock-a-doodle-do!" in English. The roosters are keeping the hens occupied with their treasures in the grass: worms, insects, and juicy bugs. Other hens are taking dirt baths next to the painting gallery where they have made a mess. The two hens who were sitting have five new chicks. It is community chick-raising, since they do not know which mother they belong to, and they keep switching between the two hens. They are adorable, and mothering them is serious business for the new mother hens. I must go to the coop often to make sure these chicks do not get stuck in unsafe places and die.

More stormy weather, humid and hot, and now fall weather! Driving around we see the scenery is changing, and many beautiful golden wheat fields stretch out to the horizon, a welcoming change of color from the very green fields of corn and soybeans. Some great cane birds, tall and long-legged, were in the soybean fields for an insect snack. They make lovely noises in the early mornings in my fields. Sometimes, if no one is around the house, they come into my little pond that has a small flowing stream going into it and snack on one of my goldfish or perhaps a little green frog sitting on a lily pad waiting for a mosquito.

I encountered a wonderful myth about corn that is appropriate to this part of Wisconsin. It comes from Dennis Klocek—whom I have mentioned already as a scientist, modern shaman, artist, alchemist, writer, and great teacher—who retells it in his book, *Seeking Spirit Vision*.

> ... An ear of wheat or corn growing on a stem can
> either serve as seed for new plants to grow or as

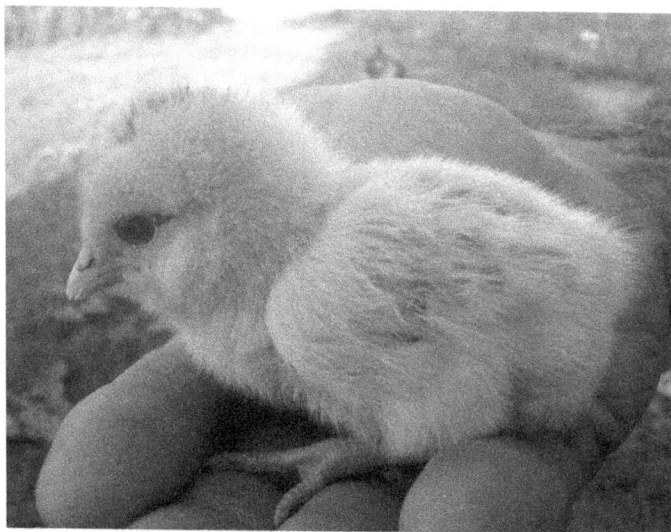

One of the chicks

nutrition for an animal or a human being. As seed it fulfills the natural evolutionary purpose of sustaining its own species, and the work of God unfolds according to divine plan. When the seed is eaten, however, the animal life which uses it for nourishment has taken it out of its natural order and used it for its own purposes. These different roles of seed in an ear of grain are reflected in aspects of the corn hero which can be traced all the way back to Cain and Abel in the Hebrew tradition. The corn hero who is broken, scattered, and buried only to rise again whole, can be meditated upon as an image of the artistic/religious creative process that involves the releasing of an idea into other levels of consciousness, forgetting and burying it, and letting it resurrect out of the womb of the total dark idea.

This image of the corn hero, however, is not useful in describing the challenges of the scientific thinker, a different kind of hero who must keep the problem close at hand and concentrate on mastering each sequential bit of data until the whole has been consumed and assimilated. The scientific thinker can then be identified with the goddess who holds all of the answers. For both types of hero the reunion with the goddess is the goal.

The artistic/religious corn hero tears himself to pieces in a self-destructive tantrum when he realizes that in order for him to be born his mother had to have a union with his father. The remorseful mother goddess gathers the pieces of the corn hero boy child and buries them. Out of the pieces, new beings are born. This type of corn hero could be called the *buried* god. The other corn hero type, the *devoured* god, is either eaten by the god or goddess or causes devouring behavior in devotees when they try to distance themselves from devotion and rituals required by the god. This type of devouring consciousness is indicative of the type of linear, sequential logic that permeates the pursuit of science. In science the thinker devours the data, bit by bit, until the thought structure becomes one with the data. The burial or gestation of the idea is not taken into account; only the devouring is important.

We can see from this that Dionysos the Elder was primarily a religious corn hero. He was torn apart, buried, and resurrected. Dionysos the Younger, however, has both the attributes of the buried corn hero and of the devoured hero. With the younger Dionysos, the corn hero is the devoured hero. With the younger Dionysos, the unconscious, mystical abandonment of ancient clairvoyance has fallen into a state of decay and drunkenness.... Dionysos the Younger is connected both to the burial initiation of ancient clairvoyance and to the awakening, devouring initiation of emerging scientific consciousness. His trial of overcoming drunkenness, or gluttony, and his trial of burial in the underworld while looking for his mother show him to be a transitional figure.

The images that arise out of such a figure as Dionysos the Younger are prophetic of a new order of hero. In art, this new hero is depicted in a different relationship to the mother. In the Egyptian figure of Isis suckling Horus, for instance, we can see that the hero is no longer in the womb. He is still dependent on the mother forces but has emerged as a separate being. The hero as a separate being is the most characteristic depiction for Madonnas in late Egyptian and Greek times. The cults of Dionysos underwent a metamorphosis from the unconscious shamanic practices of early Greece through an orgiastic phase that continued into Roman times. Dionysos the Younger had to overcome his tendency to drunken disorderliness and debauchery, and his retinue was also engaged in the trial of overcoming a bestial lower nature. The transformed Dionysos the Younger then used his newly born power of intellect to teach human beings about improved methods of agriculture, viticulture, writing and other arts. The ancient clairvoyance was thus transformed into science based on intellectual knowledge, and in the ancient world the cult of Dionysos the Younger spread throughout eastern and central Europe and Asia Minor.[40]

❧

This is the time of year for entertainment: brunch parties, luncheons, tea parties, coffee breaks, supper outside in the gardens. It is a time for friends, family, and neighbors to enjoy nature's bounty. After all the hard work of spring and early summer, the gardens are ready to be strolled in, admired, tasted, meditated upon, talked about, talked to, wondered at, and thanked. While doing all these things, elemental beings are released. Every time one notices a flower, that little elemental is released and can go on its way, so it is of great importance to notice and be thankful for all that we have—flowers, rocks, and animals alike.

I always put special rocks throughout the farm for people to notice, and I hope they do. Perhaps they can take a flower or a pebble in their hand and look at it quietly. They can practice what Michael Lipson talks about in his *Stairway of Surprise*, which will help the individual enjoy life in the garden even more. It is a book on meditation. One must do the simple exercises described in his book. What I quote is just an example. His little book of 127 pages contains steps from thinking, to doing, to feeling, to loving, to opening, to

40. Dennis Klocek, *Seeking Spirit Vision: Essays on Developing Imagination* (Fair Oaks, CA: Rudolf Steiner College Press, 1998), pp. 49–52.

thanking. This exercise is about opening. It is like homeopathy in writing, small but incredibly powerful, as is its writer who is a famous clinical psychologist.

> Steiner says that we don't perceive all we could in the physical world because of the "counterkick" of our own ideas. That is, we are continually projecting our habitual concepts onto the world about us. The world is beaming its high meanings in our direction, and we kick against them with the whole conceptual structure derived from our language, culture, and upbringing. Dissolving this structure for moments will not make us impractical dreamers or turn us into imbeciles, capable only of dumb wonder. Our familiar conceptual structure snaps back into place all too quickly. But for moments, for brief periods of practice, we can allow a little more dumb wonder into our lives. We will not suffer by it.

> Take a hard, natural object, like a stone, a twig, or a shell. It is good to work with hard objects, because they last over many days of practice. It is good to work with natural objects, because the goal is to deepen perception in the direction of nature's own ideas, and man-made objects (composed, of course, of natural elements) only distract us with the human ideas stamped into them. It should not be a particularly beautiful object, and certainly not one with sentimental associations.

> Set your object on a table or chair arm beside you and look at it in detail for thirty seconds or so. Notice its surface, its texture, the marks on it, and

its overall shape. You will see that there are no *words* for most of what you perceive of its details— subtle differences in color or contour. Yet there are *concepts*: *this* bit looks *this* way. You have a conceptual lock on every aspect of what you are seeing.

Now close your eyes for a moment to reorient yourself. Your next look will be very different. You will open your eyes briefly and just take in the stone as a whole—all of it at once, with its details, but no longer enumerating them to yourself one after the other. Open your eyes and do this whole seeing for about ten seconds.[41]

Then Michael goes on to describe more detailed exercises to train one's thinking. This way one remains with what is there. Or takes the bull by the horns! No more, no less. The book is totally unassuming, but it is a real diamond from an expert meditant who has studied with several masters, one of them Georg Kühlewind, and practiced for over 30 years. Michael Lipson also gives retreats and looks like a monk. If one practices the exercise described in his book, one can truly start to enjoy nature and life by getting rid of the non-essentials which crowd our lives.

❧

The sunset is warming the sky with soft sienna-carmine, and high up above, the clouds are catching the last light of the sun's reflections in feathery vermilion-hued forms, and

41. Michael Lipson, *Stairway of Surprise: Six Steps to a Creative Life* (Great Barrington, MA: Anthroposophic Press, 2002), pp. 101–102.

it is time to close the chicken coop and collect some Chinese hyssop leaves for a cup of tea.

The next morning is very cool, and mowing the paths in the garden is a delight. The burgundy-colored lilies are my favorites today, and I watch them from different angles to catch their glorious colors. With the sun at their backs, they reflect the colors, light beams bounce on their centers, and the colors are like a rich glass of aged-burgundy wine in the sunshine. And when I look at them in front of the light, the petals become translucent because the light is stopped by the petal and becomes enlightened matter. The matter of the petal is an angelic form, ever so thin, thin as a plane actually, or spiral, as it stops the light so we can see this enlightened radiant matter. The flower radiates by stopping the light. The matter is being made radiant by the power of the light, and is a much prettier flower from that angle. That is what I am trying to achieve in the studio, using Collot D'Herbois' techniques to bring radiance into a painting. Enlightened darkness. That is also what we all try to do within our soul, to live in the darkness of matter and bring in the light. No more dense stuff. Alchemy is present in the garden everyday, and the flowers are marvelous teachers.

Valerian has reached its peak and its strong smell, which can give one a headache, is slowly leaving the garden, while the light plant is standing tall and lanky over the other plants. They seem to say, "We are the queens of light here; let us go up, way up." It has a height contest with Queen Ann's lace. But it is much lighter, not earthly at all, and it seems to touch another realm, with its flowers that grow opposite each other on the stem until the very top flowers.

Valerian concentrates phosphorus, which is a vital constituent of plants, particularly the leaf, as it is involved in attracting the light used in photosynthesis. Preparation 507 (from biodynamic farming) stimulates the phosphate process and mobilises the phosphate-activating bacteria in the soil. Notice the connection between phosphorus, which burns with a white light, and the white valerian flowers. The flowers have a beautiful perfume. Valerian also brings the Saturn influence of warmth.[42]

This evening I will collect the flowers before they are past their peak, which will be this week, to make the preparation. But now Yarrow is coming into its own, perhaps the opposite of our friend Valerian. Yarrow is stronger, a very tough plant which is under the influence of Venus (copper-warmth carrier) and thrives in difficult conditions. The little umbrella-shaped flower is itself made of tiny flowers, all very compact. The gesture is to pack as many flowers as possible into the tiniest space, and as much essence and warmth and sun as possible, too.

Take some yarrow … This yarrow is actually a miracle of creation. So is any other plant of course, but if you compare yarrow to any other plant, you will be deeply touched by the particular wonder of yarrow. I told you how the spirit uses sulfur to moisten its fingers when it wants to carry substances—carbon, nitrogen, and so on—to their proper organic destinations. Well, the way yarrow appears in nature, it is as if some plant-designer had used an ideal

42. Proctor, *Grasp the Nettle: Making Biodynamic Farming and Gardening Work*, p. 79.

model in bringing sulfur into relationship with the other plants, the nature spirits reach the height of perfection in their use of sulfur. And if yarrow is brought into the realm of biological activity in the right way, its effect within the animal or human organism is to correct weakness of the astral body. If we know this, we can trace the essence of yarrow still further, throughout the process of plant growth in nature. Yarrow is already a great asset when it grows wild in the country, along paths, or at the edge of fields where grain, potatoes, or other crops are being grown. Of course, it should not be allowed to become a nuisance, but it is never actually harmful, so under no circumstances should you try to eradicate it. Like some sympathetic people in human society who exert and influence just by their presence, and not by what they say, yarrow's mere presence in areas where it grows abundantly is extremely beneficial....[43]

I hear shooting from the neighbor's farm and that always makes me nervous. I hope they are not shooting toward my sheep or cows. They are probably getting ready for hunting. We have many deer that help themselves to the food growing in the fields. They jump in front of cars at sunset, and we must all be careful not to hit them. They are beautiful creatures with lovely eyes; the Persian expression "deer eyes" is a wonderful poetic image.

For several years now I have been trying to tell the hunter-friends to bring the bladder of the stag for my preparations,

---

43. Steiner, *Agriculture,* p. 94.

but I have not succeeded. I will just have to go hunting myself up in the Canadian Rockies.

> ... A stag is beautiful because it stands in intense communication with its surroundings, because it directs some of its force-stream outward and lives at one with its environment and thereby takes in everything that influences the nerves and senses on an organic level. A stag thus becomes a quick and nervous animal.[44]

> ... A deer is a creature that is intimately related, not so much to the Earth as to the Earth's surroundings— to the cosmic aspect of the Earth's surroundings. That is why deer have antlers.... What is present in yarrow is especially strongly preserved in the bodies of humans and animals by means of the process that takes place between the kidneys and the bladder. And this process is dependent on the material constitution of the bladder. As thin as it may be in terms of substance, in terms of its forces a deer bladder is almost a replica of the cosmos. A deer is involved with forces that are quite different from those of a cow, which are all related to the interior. By putting the yarrow into a deer bladder, we significantly enhance its inherent ability to combine sulphur with other substances.[45]

From these insights we can see how very far one can go into the understanding of nature which surrounds us, and the only difference is that, "... handling yarrow in the way

44. Ibid., p. 71.
45. Ibid., p. 96.

I have indicated is thus a fundamental means for improving manure—and one that always stays within the living realm. It's important to note that we never get into inorganic chemistry; everything stays within the realm of the living."[46]

❧

The farm where I buy my milk is a biodynamic farm which has been applying these compost preparations for over 50 years, and the milk which comes from the cows grazing on that land has immense life forces and is thereby excellent for our children and ourselves. When we moved from New Hampshire, I told my husband I would not move to an area which did not have a biodynamic farm, and we were fortunate to find a hospital which he liked in an area which had such a farm so I could still feed my children correctly.

The family on the biodynamic farm has regular weekends where they make preparations, some of which I have made myself on our farm. But I find that I cannot do all these preparations alone, along with all my other tasks. A few years past, I had made all the preparations and was storing them in the basement. My son decided to clean out the basement, and he threw two years of work on the front lawn, including the oak bark that I had stored there after removing it from the bull's head. That was a disaster, and since then I have not had the heart to do it all over again.

I am waiting for the time when people can come and work in a cooperative way, but in the meantime, I can order the preparations. It is still much more fun to make them. In doing so the farmer becomes a healer, uniting science and

---

46. Ibid., p. 96.

Making biodynamic preparations

religion, or heaven and earth, with the help of the plants and the animals which live on the farm. I sincerely hope that more young people will become this type of farmer. The difficulty is making enough money to survive in our materialistic society where food has become a commodity rather than something sacred. We need people who have the funds—that is those of us who eat the products of the farm—to subsidize them. There is a farming community in Wilton, New Hampshire which works extremely well under these guidelines. Lincoln Geiger, Anthony Graham, and Trauger Groh work with the assistance of many young German apprentices and their wives and companions. After more than 25 years of operation, one can visit their farming community and observe how they run the farms financially. When I was part of this initiative, during the late 1980s until we moved to Wisconsin in 1997, every spring we had a meeting prior to Easter, when all the people who subscribed to the farm were shown the expenses of running the farm on a blackboard. Over the winter, the farmers calculated how much they would need to run the farm and their personal lives. The budget was then announced. For example, if the figure is, hypothetically, $200,000 dollars, then everyone declares how much money they will donate for the year. I might raise my hand and say I can give $1000.00, and so on, until all the members—at least 120 families—have spoken. All is recorded on a computer, added up, and we come to a figure, $190,000. Then we go around again until we meet the budget, then and there. The farmers get what they need for the year. People pay what they can; the ones who have more can give more voluntarily and the ones who have less give less. Everyone is happy, and everyone receives vegetables all year by coming once a week to pick them up. One can also purchase yogurt, eggs, cheese, and meat for an extra cost. This type of community supported agriculture is the way of the future. The farmers need the community and we need good pure food. With this kind of community organization, preparations such as the ones Rudolf Steiner indicated can be made as a community during festival celebrations or weekend get-togethers. I am only a flower and herb gardener and gatherer, trying hard to be a farmer because the land demands that I take care of it properly. I hope that in the future we can have a community supported arrangement here in Wisconsin, but I must wait for the young farmers to show up and lease our farm.

I mowed a large area so the chickens can happily scratch the ground for insects. The roosters are wonderful to watch, as they take their job providing for their hens seriously. The rooster is one of the animals which I think has an ego like we do—the ego of all the hens— because the hens do run without a head. He stands tall when he struts next to the other rooster saying, "I am the boss here, look at me." He stretches his wings, stands on one leg, and looks around for competition. He seems to stretch all the way to the sun because he is a sun bird. He jumps on one of his favorite concubines; her back does not have any more feathers. The other unruly teenage hens are busy laying their eggs everywhere in my garden, so the roosters can't catch them. I am trying to bring some kind of order into my chicken coop by closing the door to their small enclosure, but lately I have found the door pushed open. Today I found the culprit! The stallion has been going inside trying to eat their corn and oats. Tomorrow I will tie the door and then see what happens. A mother hen was hiding in the grass with her three little chicks, and I had to give her separate water and food. The other day I left the door opened to the special quarters for sitting hens, and one hen left her eggs and went into the main chicken coop to sit on some other eggs. Her eggs got cold, but I put her back on them, hoping they will hatch. Warmth is crucial to them; it is their life, as it is ours—inner as well as outer warmth. We underestimate the importance of inner warmth and where it comes from. Dr. Von Zabern, a scholar and our family's anthroposophic doctor when we lived in New Hampshire, recommended this lecture cycle by Rudolf Steiner, and it has become one of my favorites.

> Think of a man whose very soul is fired with enthusiasm for a high moral ideal, for the ideal of generosity, of freedom, of goodness, of love, or whatever it may be. He may also feel enthusiasm for examples of the practical expression of these ideals. But nobody can conceive that the enthusiasm which fires the soul penetrates into the bones and muscles as described by modern physiology or anatomy. If you really take counsel with yourself, however, you will find it quite possible to conceive that when a man has enthusiasm for a high moral ideal, this enthusiasm has an effect upon the warmth-organism—there, you see, we have come from the realm of the soul into the physical!

> Taking this as an example, we may say: Moral ideals come to expression in an enhancement of warmth in the warmth-organism. Not only is one warmed in soul through what he experiences in the way of moral ideals, but he becomes organically warmer as well—though this is not so easy to prove with physical instruments. Moral ideals, then, have a stimulating, invigorating effect upon the warmth-organism.

> You must think of this as a real and concrete happening: enthusiasm for a moral ideal—stimulation of the warmth-organism. There is more vigorous activity in the warmth-organism when the soul is fired by a moral ideal. Neither does this remain without effect upon the rest of man's constitution. As well as the

warmth-organism he also has the air-organism. He inhales and exhales the air; but during the inbreathing and outbreathing process the air is within him. It is of course inwardly in movement, in fluctuation, but equally with the warmth-organism it is an actual air-organism in man. Warmth, quickened by a moral ideal, works in turn upon the air-organism, because warmth pervades the whole human organism, pervades every part of it. The effect upon the air-organism is not that of warming only, for when the warmth, stimulated in the warmth-organism, works upon the air-organism, it imparts something that I can only call a source of light. Sources of light, as it were, are imparted to the air-organism, so that moral ideals which have a stimulating effect upon the warmth-organism produces sources of light in the air-organism. To external perception and for ordinary consciousness these sources of light are not in themselves luminous, but they manifest in man's astral body. To begin with, they are curbed through the air-organism that is within man. They are, so to speak, still dark light, in the sense that the seed of a plant is not yet the developed plant. Nevertheless man has a source of light within him through the fact that he can be fired up with enthusiasm for moral ideals, for moral impulses....

Think of all the experiences in your life that came from aspiration for moral ideas—or that they attracted you merely as ideas, or that you saw them coming to expression in others, or that you felt inwardly satisfied by having put such impulses into practice, by letting your deeds be fired by moral ideals.... All this goes down into the air-organism as a source of light, into the fluid organism as a source of tone, into the solid organism as a source of life. These processes are withdrawn from the field of man's consciousness but they operate within him nevertheless....

You will now begin to have an inkling of what the life that pervades the universe really is. Where are the sources of life? They lie in that which quickens those moral ideals which fire man with enthusiasm. We come to the point of saying to ourselves that if today we allow ourselves to be inspired by moral ideals, these will carry forth life, tone and light into the universe and will become world-creative. We carry out into the universe world-creative power, and the source of this power is the moral element.[47]

For more, read *The Bridge Between Universal Spirituality and the Physical Constitution of Man.* What is my ideal? What am I putting into the world? Nothing is simple. One must meditate on these words for a while before their meaning suddenly becomes clear. As my Dutch friend, Yanny would say, "Vow!"

---

47. Rudolf Steiner, "The Moral as the Source of World-Creative Powers," Lecture in Dornach Dec. 18, 1920, in *The Bridge Between Universal Spirituality and the Physical Constitution of Man* (Great Barrington, MA: SteinerBooks, 1958).

❧

This morning my guests arrive for breakfast, ladies, two of them young mothers with their little one-year-old baby girls. They are delightful and enjoy the garden as they sit down for a picture-taking session at the eastern corner of the garden. I was not surprised that they chose this area. I just mowed it and now it is becoming very lively, a lovely circular area facing the whole garden and the house in the distance. As I had walked into the garden the day before, I found this little area very warm, reassuring, and peaceful. It has always been here, but now with this clearing and mowing, it feels open and alive. The young women took this particular spot to sit and put the little babies on the ground, little angels still, and they looked perfect there. I had put a statue of an angel in this place, and it seems to belong here rather than where it had been before. So now there is a new area of the garden. I think that a Deva is most definitely here, perhaps the one who oversees the whole garden. I do not see the Deva in my mind's eye, but I feel its presence, just like these mothers knew this was the place to put their little ones and enjoy the flower beds. There is no need to say anything, but just pay attention and enjoy. I find that the less one says, the better, as these beings do not like words.

> Attention is an independent force which will not be manipulated by one's part. Cleared of all internal noise, conscious attention is an instrument which vibrates, like a crystal at its own frequency. It is free to receive the signals broadcast at each moment from a creative universe in communication with all

creatures.... Attention is the quintessential medium
to reveal man's dormant energies to himself ...[48]

To everything that man undertakes he must give his
undivided attention, his self; once he has done this,
miraculously thoughts arise, or new kinds of perceptions, which appear to be nothing more than delicate,
abrupt movements of colored pencils, or strange
contractions and figurations of an elastic fluid ...[49]

As I walk in the garden admiring the flowers, it suddenly
occurs to me that I have to make a phone call about my car
at the garage, but I do not have the phone number, so I need
to go back to the house. I return to the house and, as I stum-
ble through my disorganized address book, the phone rings.
It is the mechanic, telling me that the car is ready!

Then I step into the garden again and decide that this
little area needs one of my little dwarf statues, which had
been buried in another area in the tall, tall prairie grass
where one cannot see him. Now he has a new home in this
quiet space in the pleasant grass with his friend the protect-
ing angel, waiting for more little children! Quite a few come
roaming through the garden during the spring and summer
months. I actually made this garden for them. I tell them
that they are entering Magic Land and they must look and
listen! These children will remember this garden when they

---

48. William Segal, quoted in Astrid Fitzgerald, *An Artist's Book of Inspiration: A Collection of Thoughts on Art, Artists, and Creativity* (Great Barrington, MA: Lindisfarne Books, 1996), p. 51.

49. Novalis, quoted in Astrid Fitzgerald, *An Artist's Book of Inspiration: A Collection of Thoughts on Art, Artists, and Creativity* (Great Barrington, MA: Lindisfarne Books, 1996), p. 51.

are older, and they will in turn become gardeners. If children never see a garden, how can they become gardeners?

The masterpiece in the garden today is Purple Cone Flower, or Echinacea. It stands very tall in the garden and of course just seeds itself wherever it wants to be, which is fine with me. The beautiful color, magenta-lilac with a fantastic spiral sienna-brown madder center, sits on an extremely sturdy, hardy stem with luscious leaves. Everyone loves to look at its center, which shows a mesmerizing and prickly orange-sienna light green spiral. This spiral is called a logarithmic spiral, and one needs to do some projective geometry to understand it. *Sunspace*, by Olive Whicher,[50] one of my favorite books, includes wonderful exercises to practice. I did every one of these exercises more than once and loved them. One can go very far in understanding plants in this manner, and the doing is also healing to ourselves. None of it can be explained by words, only by practice.

The Purple Cone Flower is indeed a great plant, which loves the heartland. It is one of the main healing plants people use for building up their immune systems. One can take in the sturdiness of the plant, its strength, by watching it. People use the roots as well as the flower for medicinal purposes, but I just look at it and throw the seeds all over the place. It is tough to the touch, reflecting its ability to survive in this climate, which can be very dry; but besides its toughness, it is beautiful and sympathetic to the eye. The dried flower seeds are extremely prickly, thereby its name Echinos, from the Greek word for sea urchin.

---

50. Olive Whicher, *Sunspace: Science at a Threshold of Spiritual Understanding* (London: Rudolf Steiner Press, 1989).

Echinacea in the garden

Native Americans used Echinacea extensively. In fact, American Indians used it more than any other plant in the treatment of illness and injury. The root was used externally for the healing of wounds, burns, abscesses, and insect bites; internally for infections, toothaches, and joint pains; and as an antidote to rattlesnake bites.[51]

---

51. Michael T. Murray, *The Healing Power of Herbs* (Roseville, CA: Prima Publishing, 1992), p. 19.

In the winter I often take some Echinacea essence made by our friend, local pharmacist Marc McKibben at Uriel Pharmacy, in case my body needs it to help fend off colds. I can imagine this area of southeastern Wisconsin, peopled with Native Americans in their natural homes, with beautiful fields of these Great Plains flowers that bring beauty and healing to the earth and humanity. When we first moved here, we wanted to seed the whole 30-acre meadow in front of the road with wildflowers. Perhaps I will extend the Echinacea bed a little further out into the alfalfa field.

There is nothing better than walking in the orchard by the flower garden and picking the first peaches from the trees. They taste heavenly, and every day we eagerly wait for the few peaches that have ripened slowly under the warm sun. The birds are also fond of them, so I have to beat them to it. The peaches seem to glow on the tree in red, yellow, and gold. They are refreshing and good for thinking, so I have been told. I used to tell my son when he was in college to eat lots of peaches when he took his exams. The branches are bending under the weight of its treasures, though we eat them all as soon as they are ready. Friends are also waiting for gifts of peaches, so they can make their famous pies or cobblers. My neighbor Andre has the best recipe.

> ... Just like the color of flowers, the fine taste of apricots or plums is a cosmic quality that has made its way up into the fruit. In every apple you are actually eating Jupiter; in every plum, Saturn.[52]

---

52. Steiner, *Agriculture*, p. 40.

Ripe peaches ready for harvesting

❧

The crescent moon is over the southwestern skies accompanied by bright Venus, a lovely combination in a clear sky, and we will prepare for a lunar eclipse due in a couple of weeks. The fireflies dance all night, looking like little fairies in the farm fields, gardens, and woods. They always make their appearance a week or so after St. John's Day. Children enjoy their company, wondering how they can shine like that. It is said that in the future, we will shine with our own inner light, because the outside won't have light anymore. We will shine with our own inner wisdom, our own inner sun, because the outside sun is dying. The fireflies are ahead of us; so are the phosphorescent fish deep in the ocean where there is no light.

The bees have been extremely active and it is time again to gather honey. I must sweep the garage, wash the stainless-steel honey extracting machine, and look for buckets. It is always extremely hot when we do this kind of work. My husband has to put on his winter snowsuit, and will sweat off at least five pounds while working. We have to tape his headgear and gloves on so the bees do not get in his clothing, which they invariably do. This year we have darker Russian bees and Italian bees, among others. We are trying to make the bees stronger so they will survive. Bees are dying everywhere, because they have become weaker due to abuse, and they cannot fend off parasites, tiny mites sucking them. Hopefully, on this farm they are gathering strength again because we do not take a lot of their honey. My husband feels that when we take the honey, it is as if we were cutting their legs and arms, so to speak. We see the bees everywhere in my flower gardens and drinking from our flowforms and pond where I put stones on the sides so they can sit and drink. We love the honey; I use at least one or two tablespoons a day. It has lots of energy gathered from the bees' summer flights. They especially love the thyme flower beds.

On warm days when there is a flurry of activity, we see the bees with yellow nectar on their tiny legs, flying back and forth from their hives, and we know that all is well. They add much to the farm; we could not do without them.

And what of honey?

Plants, we know, refine their starches into sugar found in their blossoms, and then further etherealize their substance into scent, radiant colour and wafting pollen. The further this sublimation has progressed, the more spiritualized are the substances involved, but the less alive ...

The honey stored in blossoms is therefore a very special substance. Though it has still not quite left the life-realm, it also has to do with the salt sphere—the salt we described as possessing wisdom. But honey's special quality is its closeness to the spirit, for it is produced in the area where plant substance is refined and metamorphosed into spiritual formative forces. It is both a physical and spiritual substance, permeated by salt's wisdom, which at this stage is closely related to the carrying quality of cosmic thought.

'Salt' in this context is not to be confused with root salts.... The spiritual salt process in the plant is therefore not the same thing as earthly, mineral salt, but consists of finely dispersed blossom elements, such as nectar, scent, colour, and pollen.

The bees carry the nectar they gather into their selfless sphere, where everything is governed by a wise group-ego. People really able to appreciate the wisdom in a beehives' organization will sense a connection here with the human future. The fact that the temperature in a beehive is exactly that of human blood points to the activity in it of a co-coordinating ego similar to man's. And the wise will see in the bee's overcoming of sexuality, the pattern of developments to come.

Bees live in the world's breathing process. For the blossoms that pour out colour, scent and pollen are the world's organs of outbreathing, and the wise group soul of bees has made them carriers of these substances. Honey is therefore a food that supports those human functions that help thinking to be felt and willed, and will and feeling guided by thinking. In the metabolic sphere honey stimulates the kidney action that we have found so vitally tied up with breathing and the nervous system. Indeed, honey has an ego-like capacity to work on man's organism and charge his blood with ego-like upbuilding impulses....

Work with bees makes one receptive to inspiration from the bee's group spirit. The social forms that must be created before much longer will merge, in an illumined but still distant future, into simple love of our fellow men.

Honey thus has a deep connection with man's future development, as milk has with his past. And just as milk prepared us to enter earthly incarnation, honey prepares us to leave the earth when that time comes. Honey helps us to grow old gracefully and to ripen the wise fruits of living....[53]

Dr. Hauschka's book is a must for anyone who truly wants to understand something about real nutrition, and it is good to read with his companion book, *The Nature of Substance*, which is a marvel.[54]

---

53. Hauschka, *Nutrition: A Holistic Approach*, pp. 83–85.

54. Rudolf Hauschka, *The Nature of Substance: Spirit and Matter* (London: Sophia Books/Rudolf Steiner Press, 2002).

In one more anecdote about bees, Dr. Bertrand Von Zabern, an anthroposophical doctor living in Temple in southern New Hampshire whom I have already mentioned, once told me, "Yes, if people come to you because they are ill, sometimes for some of them there is not much that can be done. That is when the bees can be very useful. You see, these people are like blocks of cement; nothing moves them. Their souls are dying—no movement, so you tell them to get stung by some bees! It is excellent; it helps invigorate them, and it wakes them up!" On the farm, we do get stung from time to time, and maybe that isn't a bad thing; the farm has a sting and zest for life. There are people who are very allergic to them, but they stay away.

❧

The young stallion is venturing further and further from the barn, which is of some concern. He is free, and now he is wandering near the house in the orchard, helping himself to apples. I hope he knows when to stop; otherwise he will get colicky and ill. My husband thinks that the horse knows instinctively what to do because of the way we have brought him up. He is not enclosed in the barn or some tiny meadow. Still, I need to keep an eye on him. If the postman comes in and forgets to close the big gate, we are in trouble. This stallion is growing into a beautiful, sweet, gentle horse. When he gets tired of an area, he gallops back into the barn or visits his friend Max, the Arab across the fence who is continually calling after him if he ventures too far from his sight.

We have another photo session in the garden, and I notice the late-blooming lilies are making their appearance. They are definitely the queens of the garden. I always forget what I plant and where, and it is a great surprise to see who shows up. The bunny has not eaten those yet, as he is busy with another plant—until he goes into the cooking pot. This late-blooming tiger lily variety looks extremely strong and sends a sweet smell over the whole area. It is growing to my height in some places, so we know the manure is working. One can feel the intensity of summer when strolling through the garden. The colors are intense, as is the activity of the bees, butterflies, and other insects. The flowers are saying: "This is our time, we do not have all year, let's try and reach up to the sun, and down to the center of the earth with our roots!"

Lily and rose can both serve as representatives of the whole plant kingdom … Each is a queen in her own realm. The two may be said to dominate the plant kingdom as sun and moon the heavens. They have been symbols of special qualities from time imme- morial and were sought after by the wise men of the orient. Zarathrustra, the great initiate of early Persian days, taught his followers to breed the food plants that we still consider most important: fruits and cereals. The first are related to the rose, the sec- ond to the lily family.

All the various lilies have the six-pointed star of Zarathrustra as their flower pattern. Tradition links lilies to the goddess Isis, and the so-called Madonna lily is a Christian version of the same. Lilies are the plant of wisdom. Where they have been bred into food plants, as in the humble onion, leek, garlic,

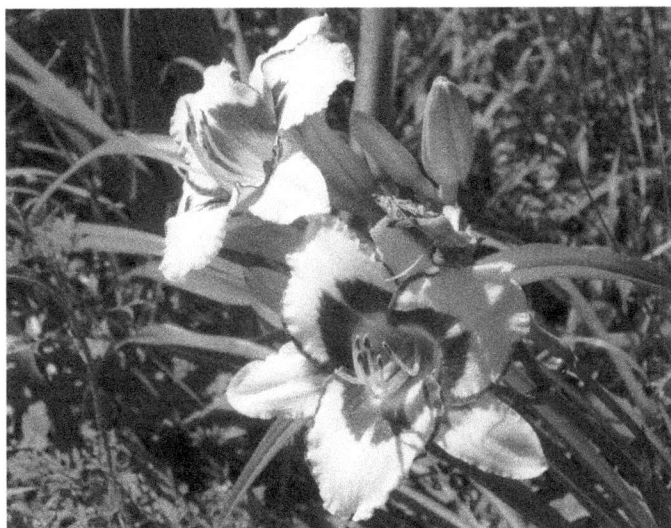

Lilies in the garden

chives, and so on, they clearly reveal their link with the nervous system. The fragrance element of the blossom process permeates the onion through and through, extending its aroma and a certain rousing sharpness down into stalk and leaf. In its shape and substance too we see clear indications of the descent of the heavenly forces through the entire plant. Thus it lends itself ideally to the role of digestive quickener. It 'aromatizes' those who partake of it, from inside out to their skin periphery. It stimulates excretion while at the same time helping soul and spirit incarnate fully. Thus it proves itself an aid to the proper functioning of the two poles in man related to moon forces: brain and regeneration.

It is no coincidence that those oriental peoples most concerned with developing the brain as the organ of earthly reason, the Chaldeans, Sumerians and Semites, are even today particularly fond of eating onions.[55]

This offers much food for thought, and it is wonderful to stroll in the garden with Dr. Hauschka's great insights.

Driving down the roads here, we see golden wheat fields. Some fields have just been harvested. The golden stalks reflect the sunrays. Looking from afar, the wheat fields shine like gold, a different feeling from the green corn and soybean fields. The wheat fields look beautiful in their golden shimmer at all times of the day, but at noon, or at sunset, they are especially peaceful and rich. They are restful to the eye after all the green.

In a narrower sense, the grasses from which grains were developed are also related to the lily family. Though breeding of true lilies developed onion forms, in the case of cereals seed-formation was the object. This has given cereal species a sun-related universality, even though they are offshoots of the lily family. They provide us with carbohydrates in the form of starches: sun-charged foods that show their universality in that grains, like all seeds, contain proteins, oils and salts. That makes our 'daily bread', practically as well as symbolically, *the* human food.

Wheat, rye, barley and oats are the grains known and grown in Central Europe [and the United States]. They are all wind-pollinated, meaning that

55. Hauschka, *Nutrition: A Holistic Approach*, p. 87.

air currents rather than insects do the work of pollination. Cosmic soul-being, active in the atmosphere and in bees, butterflies and other insects, touches plants, and they respond with a glorious wealth of colour. With grains, there is no such actual touching, but only a general mingling with the soul-like airy element. This gives cereals a special aspect, considering the goodness and wisdom inherent in the soul-being of the cosmos, which we have identified above with Isis-Madonna.[56]

Dr. Hauschka also mentions, among many other topics, that wheat is related to earth/calcium salts, that rye is related to water/potassium salts, barley to air/silicic acid, and finally, oats to fire/magnesium salts. So here, through these wonderful cereals, we see the four elements and the four temperaments. Would a choleric person—one who angers easily—eat lots of oats? Or would this person eat wheat, which is earthly and heavier? Why do we like dumplings? I love dumplings myself. Is it because they weigh one down? Think about yourself and what you like to eat and see what you discover. I am a bit of a choleric myself, and I love wheat bread.

❧

Each morning now, I walk through the orchard and gather a basket full of peaches. The orchard has a wonderful, pleasant, rich aroma and is full of birds flying from one tree to the next. The sun's rays are hitting the fruit-laden branches

56. Ibid., pp. 87–89.

with their warmth, and the fruits slowly ripen. It is not yet time for jam.

> Lilies and the cereals related to them are ... offspring of the moon principle, the regent of wisdom and governor of nerve processes. A study of the rose, however, shows that it bears the sun's signature.

> Due to the sun forces which they embody, plants of the rose family have an entirely different relationship to earth from lilies. They even grow into very large trees, bright with a glory of pentagonal blossoms in purple, rose, or white. Light and darkness intermingle in them. Red roses have the colour of irradiated blood, of darkness redeemed by complete suffusion with the light element.

> The fruits of today are all descendants of the rose. They possess nutritive qualities very different from those of cereals in that they do not build tissue but instead help body and spirit work harmoniously together.... Fruit thus nourishes our human-ness by linking our physical and our cosmic being. Its effect is felt in the life of our will and moral creativity.

> Fruit feeds the circulatory processes and even has a direct part in making blood itself. Strawberries for instance, are an excellent remedy for anemia.

> A study of the various fruits turns up many differences....

> ... [T]here are four general groups of fruits: stone-fruits, seed-bearers, haw-fruits and berries. The way

a plant sets fruit and seed always seems expressive of
its underlying character.

The cherry, one of the group of stone-fruits that
includes plums, apricots and peaches, has a single,
isolated but beautifully formed pit that hardens and
becomes a stone. The whole picture is one of self-
sufficiency, even of something not too far removed
from egotism. As though to make up for the pit's
contraction, the fruit fills out around it and is plump
and juicy....[57]

We have said that lily and rose related to each other
as nerves to blood. Since the latter are the physiolog-
ical basis of thinking and will, we can equally well
say that lily and rose resemble thinking and willing.
We are evermore compelled to infuse will into our
thinking and thought into doing. What on the physi-
ological level must be kept separate can be fruitfully
united on the soul plane. Bread and fruit are the two
foods which support such union....[58]

The chicken coop provided a pleasant surprise last night.
My husband called out and said, "The sitting hen just had
seven chicks!" I was glad, because I had left the door open
as I mentioned before, and she had gone out for a few hours,
letting her eggs get cold, but I decided to give them a chance.
I am glad I did. They survived: two yellow ones, one deep
grey, two totally black ones, and two multicolored-speckled
ones. I help them, and one must hold them because they are
irresistible. I paid them a visit several times today to make

---

57. Ibid., pp. 90–92.

58. Ibid., p. 93.

A hen with her chicks

sure they do not go in between little cracks in the henhouse and get stuck there. They will be in their own separate area for at least one week.

Eggs always remind me of my daughter who, from a very early age, loved to hold eggs. She was fascinated with eggs, so we acquired quite a collection of semi-precious stone and wooden eggs. It was a love at first sight, and she put the eggs in their bed, or carried some around in a handkerchief, pretending they were her children. Her dolls were not as interesting, so we bought Russian dolls with egg-like shapes. Then one day she saw an ostrich egg and had to have it, but it was too expensive. She had to wait another few years before we eventually bought the egg, but by then she was older and had other interests. The archetypal form of the oval egg is healing—the cosmic egg—and for a toddler it was the best toy. When she was ten, we went hiking in Isle de

Haut, Maine, where there are beaches with rocks that look like eggs, softly shaped by the sea. There she found an enormous rock in the shape of an egg, bigger than an ostrich egg, and she brought it back to the mainland, although it was quite heavy. Now it sits in my kitchen with a small, Chinese fisherman holding a fishing rod glued to it.

The Earth as it circles the Sun makes the shape of an egg, the elliptical journey, the sliced egg. If we think of that as an enormous egg shape in time-space, we have an egg. Small children always know best; they are still connected with the cosmos.

The weekend is here and if the weather holds, I will be sitting on the tractor making the second cut of the hay field. I also need to start gathering more herbs from the garden. The sage plants are doing very well here, seeding themselves so that I can replant them elsewhere. I use a lot of sage tea in the winter, as it is excellent for warding off colds. I gather a lot of sage for drying and to give to friends who are sick with colds or flu, so they can make a tea with the leaves, adding some honey for sweetness.

Here is a good sage recipe: Take a bunch of sage leaves (dry or fresh), and fry them with onions in olive oil until golden. Then add fresh or frozen tomatoes and salt. Let everything simmer for a while covered. This makes an excellent tomato soup.

Now is not the time for this, however, since my tomatoes are still ripening and the rabbit is eating them as soon as they are ready.

The ancient Greeks valued sage highly and in Britain the Druids believed that a potion made with the herb could revive the dead. It must be admitted, though, that sage should be used with discretion; just two leaves placed inside a roast duck will perfume the whole carcass during cooking.[59]

Zucchinis are now plentiful. This is the time when I look up recipes to serve this vegetable in different ways because I have so much of it, as does everyone else. The other day I baked it with the badly behaved teenage chickens who ended up in our freezer, plus some oregano and oil. Simple cooking is the best. Here is Geraldene Holt's recipe, which is new to me, but similar to my husband's Persian eggplant dish. *Courgettes aux feuilles de coriander* sounds better than "zucchini with fresh coriander."

The influence of the North African countries is still felt in French cooking. A herb much used in Middle-Eastern cooking, coriander, is here mixed with ginger and yogurt to sharpen the slightly bland taste of the zucchini.

Serves 4

1 lb of zucchini
walnut-sized piece of fresh ginger, peeled and grated
salt
2 tbsp. of butter
1-2 tsp. of chopped fresh coriander (cilantro) leaves
⅔ cup of creamy whole milk yogurt

Wipe the zucchini with a damp cloth. Slice thinly and place in a colander or a Chinese steaming

---

59. Geraldene Holt, *Recipes from a French Herb Garden* (NY: Simon and Schuster, 1989), p. 96.

> basket. Sprinkle the grated ginger on top and
> steam until cooked.

Turn the zucchini into a hot serving dish, season
> with salt and keep warm. Melt the butter in a
> pan and mix in the coriander leaves and the
> yogurt, stirring for 1-2 minutes until hot but
> not boiling. Pour sauce over the zucchini and
> serve.[60]

Another recipe, which I will use for my peaches, is peach pie with hyssop as a flavoring herb and hazelnuts in the crust (Holt, p. 142). A custard flavored with peach leaves is another new recipe for my "magic cooking repertoire" (Holt, p. 140). There are more wonderful recipes in a cookbook by Susan Cadogan and illustrated beautifully by Elizabeth Auer called *The Community Cooks*.[61] I wrote several recipes in it along with others in the community in Southern New Hampshire that is centered around the Pine Hill Waldorf School in Wilton.

Enough about cooking or this will turn into a cookbook, but living on the farm with large gardens and orchards we are always looking for recipes. It is part of life in the country. While many people move to Europe, especially Southern France, Italy or Spain, I think we can find our way back to the land here as well. All it takes is care and work. People need to leave the large cities and create small farms. This movement has started already, but we need it to happen on a very large scale before all the land is swallowed up by developers who are building business parks by the hundreds of

---

60. Ibid., p. 121.

61. Susan Cadogan, *The Community Cooks* (Townsend, MA: Amazon Publications, 1990).

thousands or mansion parks where 5000- to 6000-square-foot houses sit next to another one. Here one can see the ravaged landscape. On this entire road I am the only one who has a variety of animals and large perennial gardens. One small farm has calves they raise for meat in a small area, and one neighbor has a small vegetable garden. There are 10 residences on this four-mile-long road, and several farms have been converted to soybean and corn fields, hay, wheat, and oats, but there are no more cows. Large barns sit empty and dead. But go another 10 miles down the road, and one can see enormous milking farms exploiting the cows to the maximum. Some of them have 1500 cows, and the cows never go out, but stay in one place where they are fed. Their veterinary hospital is larger than the farms, with 100 or so sick animals at any given time.

People drink the milk, eat the cheese and ice cream from these cows, and wonder why they are getting sick and fat. There are many books available on this topic. That is another reason for having this small farm with many animals; it reminds people driving through here on the weekends that animals belong on the land. They are beautiful to look at and perhaps some will decide to change their lifestyle.

There are other reasons for us to do what we are doing on our farm:

> ... [I]t is important to not keep animals confined in dark stalls where no cosmic forces can reach them, but to let them out to pasture and give them opportunities to interact with their surroundings through their senses. Just picture an animal in some dark and airless building, standing in front of a feeding trough that contains whatever human wisdom has

doled out. If it never has the opportunity to be out-doors, this animal will be very different from an animal that can roam freely and use its senses—its sense of smell, for instance—seek out the cosmic forces. It will be very different from an animal that actively searches for its own food. The animal left in front of the trough will not immediately show that it has no more cosmic forces; it still inherits some, but this deficiency will gradually become apparent in its descendants. These animals will become weak because of their head; that is, they will not be able to nourish their bodies because they will be unable to absorb the cosmic substances that their bodies require. These things will show you that what is important is not to come up with generalities about what to feed in this or that instance, but rather to understand what value particular feeding methods have for the animal's entire being and constitution.[62]

We got more rain when we needed it, and now we have a beautiful weekend. We started mowing the second hay cut and now we are finishing it up. I spent more time driving the enormous, powerful tractor. It is bee time as well, and we are harvesting the honey. My husband put on his bee out-fit—the surgeon outfit this time, not the skiing one—and went to handle the three big hives by the sheep barn. He smoked them with some tansy flowers, but they were not dry enough, so he switched to dry apple wood. The bees became disoriented and gave him no grief, not even one sting. He processed the honey in the garage. It is always a miracle to see that magic, thick liquid pouring into big buckets. We

---

62. Steiner, *Agriculture*, p. 156.

Processing honey

only took three buckets and left the other supers stacked up on the hive, full of honey, as the ratio should be only 20 percent. We could have gotten much more, but it would have been a shock to the hive. Commercial beekeepers put their bees under a lot of stress and we try to help the situation by not overworking our hives. I looked at the supers full of honey and noticed the cells where the queens were being developed; there were quite a few of them. Then I saw some of the drones, which have heavier behinds.

... [C]osmic influences have a tremendous effect upon the beehive. You would be able to gain a correct and true understanding of life within the beehive if you were to allow for the fact that everything in the environment that surrounds the Earth in all directions has an extremely strong influence on what goes on in the beehive ... The bees have a life in which that element is suppressed, very strongly suppressed, which in other animals is expressed through their sexual life....

You see, with bees it is always the case that only very few chosen females, the queen bees, take care of all the propagation of the species. With the rest, the sexual life is more or less repressed, but in this sexual life there is another element—love life—which is, above all, a matter concerning the soul. Only when the soul element works on certain organs of the body do these organs become a manifestation, an expression of love life. Since this love life is held back in all the bees except a single queen, the sexual life of the beehive is transformed into all this activity that the bees develop among themselves. That is why those much older and wiser people of a time long ago, "knew" about this in a very different way than the way we know things today; they knew that the wonderful activity of the beehive pointed back to the condition of the bees' love life, the love life that these people associated in their minds with the planet Venus.

... That which we experience within ourselves only at a time when our hearts develop love is actually the very same thing that is present as a substance in the entire beehive. The whole beehive is permeated with life based on love. In many ways the bees renounce love, and thereby this love develops within the entire beehive. You'll begin to understand the life of bees once you're clear about the fact that the bee lives as if it were in an atmosphere pervaded thoroughly by love.

But the thing that a bee profits from the most is that it derives its sustenance from the very parts of a plant that are pervaded by the plant's love life. The bee sucks its nourishment, which it makes into honey, from the parts of a plant that are steeped in love life. And the bee, if you could express it this way, brings love life from the flowers into the beehive....

... The bee, with the exception of the queen bee, is a being that would say, if I may put it this way: "As individuals we want to renounce all sexual life, so that we make each one of us into a supporter of the hive's love life." They have indeed carried into the hive that which lives in the flowers. When you begin to think through all of this properly, you will have unlocked the whole secret of the beehive. The living element of this thriving, germinating love that is spread out over the flowers is also contained in the honey the bees make.

You can study this matter further by eating the honey. What does the honey do? ... Honey creates sensual pleasure, at the most, on the tongue. At the moment when you eat honey, it creates the proper connection and relationship between the airy and fluid elements in the human being. There is nothing better for a human being than to add a little honey in the right quantity to food....

... Whenever someone adds honey to food, that person wants to prepare the soul element for properly working upon the body, for breathing, as it were. This is why beekeeping can be a great aid to human culture; it makes human beings strong ...[63]

After four days of cleaning, gardening, and cooking up a storm, we celebrated the gathering of honey by inviting some friends for a garden dinner party. There were eight of us enjoying a sunny evening while a pleasant breeze kept away the bugs. Everyone tasted the new bees' magic nectar in our fresh mint tea. In the late evening the full moon showed her face on the eastern sky among feathery crimson clouds, and it was time to say good-bye. But first we gathered by the great big grandfather tree and acknowledged its beauty and wondrous strength. My husband had to catch Max, the Arab, who had escaped from his field where the beehives are. We had left the door open to work on the bees.

🌿

It is Sunday, the cock is singing, and the noise of the tractor fills the warm air. The fields are almost all cut and will dry during the next few days, as there is no rain in sight. August

63. Rudolf Steiner, *Bees: Lectures by Rudolf Steiner*, Lecture in Dornach February 3, 1923 (Great Barrington, MA: Anthroposophic Press, 1998), pp. 2–4.

is approaching, the flowers are in full bloom, and I have a few more days of transplanting and gardening to do.

Wisconsin is in full-time summer recreational activity mode. Horse shows are everywhere, and summer outdoor theaters are in full schedule. We always dedicate a couple of weekends to outdoor Shakespearean plays, which we love. Over the last ten years we have grown very fond of the actors and actresses; we feel we grow with them. So much work, dedication, and talent are a great addition to our summer life in these Wisconsin hills, especially at Spring Green, home of Frank Lloyd Wright.

The farmers have no time for playing. They work constantly on their farms, fields, barns, and gardens, but they do make time for large picnic gatherings of family and friends, and enjoy receiving the public on their large farms for public breakfasts. When not working, they get their animals ready for the local county fairs where everyone enjoys seeing people show off their well-taken-care-of prizewinning animals.

Many also gravitate to the many Wisconsin lakes for boating, waterskiing, sailing, or gathering to eat and drink on pontoon boats or picnicking by the water. Bikers too, both men and women on large motorcycles, take long drives on country roads, stopping at local bars for beer, enjoying the wind in their faces and the scenery. Bicyclists and runners exercise on the country roads as well. There is a small airplane crowd that flies between the many little airports which dot the Midwest. One can look at the sky on a pleasant afternoon and see all kinds of airplanes, plus occasional skydivers and a few hot-air balloons, which invariably fly very low right over my bedroom's skylight when I am still sleeping. I imagine that they will one day land on the big grandfather tree.

The Walworth County Fair

We have many wonderful horse shows at this time of year featuring English riders, Western riders, and teams of all sorts. The roads are full of horse trailers taking these magnificent animals to the dozens of events that take place every weekend. The workhorse teams are a pleasure to watch at fair time. My favorite fair is called the Walworth County Fair, and I never miss it. It is a little bit of the true American Wild West living in these Wisconsin hills. That is the spirit that I truly enjoy here. Many are still in contact with the earth and the animals, and it shows. But if land is being sold more and more for subdivisions and business parks, the farmers will not have money for land or farming. Then we will truly lose the spirit of the West, and that will bring the death of the soul. For now, however, this is still an area for workhorse breeders as well as sheep farmers, although there are many big pig-producing and cattle-breeding operations, too.

It is late evening, and the freshly cut field sends its aroma of alfalfa and timothy grass into the cool evening air. The chickens are in their coop, the seven brand new chicks are nicely tucked away under mother hen after a long day of running around in the fields. The horses are upset because my husband went for a ride with China, Aryan, and the German shepherd and left them alone. The sheep are going out for a late evening snack under the very fat crimson full moon which is slowly rising on the eastern horizon, right over the neighbor's large barn like a big ball of fire, and facing the moon are the carmine western skies announcing a hot day tomorrow. The birds have quieted their raucous singing, and all is quiet in the Wisconsin hills, except for the singing frogs sitting on the lily pad in their ponds. Night is slowly settling in. Tomorrow I will help a friend pollinate corn for a couple of hours. That wondrous plant is getting ripe and I think this year will be an abundant year, since there was no lack of sun or rain here!

Tragedy has struck our little community. One of our eldest has had a stroke. I went to visit Mrs. Martina Mann at the hospital to try and bring some warmth to a cold hospital setting. She is valiant and strong in spirit. We all hope that she will regain her strength and enjoy her grandchildren for a few more years. Things get shaken up, and getting back to normal is difficult in these circumstances.

The weather is extremely hot. Yesterday when I was bailing hay I could not stand to be too long on the tractor. One more project and we will have finished this year's big projects. That is a great feeling, but this project is a big one: clean both the big barn and the smaller one, make compost piles which need to be treated with biodynamic preparations, and spread some of the manure on the fields.

Today I will go and help out with pollinating the corn for a couple of hours in the evening when it is cooler. The fields of corn were full of mosquitoes late in the evening, and because I was not dressed properly, I could only stay there less than an hour. The tall plants were like a cathedral. I was shown how to look for the little corn with tiny silk threads and to put an envelope on it. The next day someone would pollinate this little beginning of an ear of corn.

The peach season is almost finished. I have been eating plenty of peaches, which are rich in phosphorus, and if that is the case, I may begin to shine in the dark! The birds have enjoyed them as well.

The weather is hot, and my garden is turning into beautiful seeds. Plants are seeding everywhere and I need to collect some of these seeds for planting next year. The tomatoes are not yet red, but growing, and I have to compete with the rabbits for consumption.

The next month on the farm is always frantic. The corn needs to be frozen, tomato and zucchini sauce cooked, peach and plum jams made, and herbs dried for teas. Along with the usual gardening, irises and other plants need to be divided and transplanted, lawns mowed, and care taken of

One of the flowforms

the flowforms and ponds. My usual work of writing and watercolor painting fits in between all this, so I rarely have time for other activities—maybe a movie here and there when I can't look at another book.

The kitchen is a constant disaster, with something always cooking on the stove and its general messiness. It seems to always be around 95 degrees when I am canning my tomato sauce, and this household does not have frozen dinners; everything is made from scratch. We have lots of desserts as well, because when one works hard one gets hungry.

Sometimes when living on a farm there is great joy when winter comes. There is no more hard work, and there is a freezer and pantry full of prepared food. That is why most farmers and gardeners here in the upper Midwest, or the north in general, love the winter so they can slow down and enjoy a different lifestyle. The animals still need care, but the hay is in the barn and we just give it to them along with water. There is no more frenzy, only calm settling in for the cold months.

But now it is very hot and there is much rain. It makes work in the tomato patch difficult, as do the mosquitoes. If I lived in a city apartment, I would not know what to do with myself; I would be bored and get myself into plenty of trouble with all my energy. Somehow everything gets done, but how it does, who knows?

Last week we took a weekend away from the farm to see three plays at the Spring Green outdoor theater. Two of the plays were rained out after the second act, so we will go back in September. We biked through old train tracks and enjoyed the time-out from farm life. We visited old villages by the Wisconsin River where it joins the Mississippi. We have one more weekend planned to see some old Indian sites and their pyramidal mounds and stockade, formerly called Atzalan (1100-1200).

I just husked and cooked two dozens ears of corn and froze the delicious golden yellow kernels for winter use. The Indians worshipped the ear of corn for millennia, and with good reason.

> Deification is generally the beginning of the end, the first stage of the journey that is to lead to death. When a man is deified he dies, and similarly when an element which forms the economic basis of a nation's life is raised to the skies, it has ceased to function in its proper way. This truism has been exemplified time and time again, but nowhere in so symbolical and transfigured a fashion as among those Indians whose habitat lay between that of the Pueblo and the heirs of the Mound-Builders and whose most representative tribes was the Pawnee.

Maize, in this sign we shall conquer! Such was the battle cry of the Pawnee; conquer life materially, symbolically and ethically. And thus we find in the principal ceremony of the Pawnee, the Hako, an ear of white maize with its tip painted blue to represent the sky, the dwelling place of the spirits, and four blue equidistant lines running halfway down the ear, to symbolize the four paths along which maize is here to lead man to a revivified conception of peace and good-will.

Prefiguring the journey that is to unite father and son, in the Hako ceremony of peace—to merge the old with the new—the Great Mother, maize, consents to lead, and as the procession solemnly winds its way, a chant arises:

Mother Corn, Oh hear! Open your way!
Lo! As we draw near, let our souls touch thine
While we pray thee:
Children give to us! Mother Corn hear!

Mother Corn, Oh hear! Open your way!
Lo! Our heads we bow, while our souls touch thine;
Then as one mind
Make the choice of a Son. Mother Corn, hear!

Mother Corn, Oh hear! Open your way!
Lo! With head erect Mother stands, and then
Moves through the air
On her mission bent. Mother Corn, hear!

Mother Corn, Oh hear! Open your way!
Lo! Our journey's end now is near, we look
O'er the strange land,
Seeking children there! Mother Corn, hear!

Mother Corn, Oh hear! Open your way!
Lo! Our eyes behold where they dwell. In their
Village we walk
Seeking the Son. Mother Corn, hear!

Mother corn, Oh hear! Open your way!
Lo! His lodge we find, through the door we pass.
Sleeping he lies,
Knows not we are there. Mother Corn, hear!

Mother Corn, Oh hear! Open your way!
Lo! Now at her touch comes a dream; then a
Bird calls, "My Son!"
While his soul responds. Mother Corn, hear![64]

Here we no longer have appreciation for ritual and ceremony and must learn to celebrate again the bounty of nature, not as it was done before, but in a new way.

The economic basis of the life was maize. Like fire the worship of maize permeated every element of their life. Their main ceremony was grouped around it. Essentially this consisted of eating in common and in a religious manner, new maize which had been sown for this specific purpose. It was a solemn feast. When the maize was to be planted, a

64. Paul Radin, *The Story of the American Indian* (New York: Liveright Publishing Corporation, 1944), pp. 256–257.

new plot of earth was chosen that had not been cul-
tivated within the memory of man. This plot was
freed of all the trees and brushwood growing upon
it. Everything connected with the working of the
field and with the culture of the maize had, among
the Natchez Indians, to be done by warriors. The
smallest operations were not regarded as unworthy
of them. For any one but a warrior to have touched
the maize would have been regarded as profanation.
So sacred and revered was it that it was believed that
any person who so profaned the field, would never
be able to leave it but would perish miserably. As
soon as the stalks approached maturity, the warriors
went to the place where the maize was to be eaten
and where a kind of granary had been erected.

... [W]hen everything was disposed and prepared
for the harvest and the maize was ripe, the warriors
went to gather it. In fact the entire nation prepared
itself to participate in the great feast. At daybreak
everybody was already astir. The old men as well
as the women and children all left at sunrise. Each
one brought the utensils necessary for preparing the
grain, and, as soon as they arrived, they collected
the wood to make a fire at the proper time.[65]

In the ten years we have lived here, there has not been
a rainy season such as this. The fields are green like spring,
but it is past mid-August. And there will be more rain
today. The farmers aren't complaining, and the orchard is
very happy to have all the drink it needs, unlike the past

---

65. Ibid., p. 206.

droughty summers. Next year will be a very good year for those fruits trees.

Browsing through the Wisconsin State Farmer's newspaper, I saw a very important little article:

"White Buffalo Born on Vernon County Farm"

For the third time in recent years, a white buffalo calf has been born on a Wisconsin farm. Back in 1994 Dave and Valerie Heider had a buffalo cow that gave birth to a white calf that they named Miracle. As many Wisconsonites learned then, the birth of a white buffalo calf is so rare that it has great meaning to American Indians. During his ten years of life, Miracle was visited by thousands of American Indians ... In Sioux tribal lore the birth of a white buffalo is said to usher in a period of great change. Since 1994 there has been a white buffalo calf born every year. They take this as a great blessing but also as a warning ... (August 17, 2007)

Last winter I read about the important birth of a white lioness in Africa in the book *The Mystery of the White Lions*, by Linda Tucker. What she found in her intensive research correlates with what the Indian elders in these ancient Midwestern grounds are also saying about the white buffalo. I am quoting a very large passage, but her words are very potent.

The more I had delved, the more I myself had come to believe in the luminous Sun God qualities of the White Lions. I truly believe in the luminous Sun God qualities of the White Lions. I truly believe them to be guardian angels of sorts. Nothing was more important to me than honoring the truth, which was progressively being unearthed in respect to these unique creatures. If I truly had a part to play as custodian of the White Lions on earth, I was prepared to spare nothing in honoring the true gold which I saw reflected in them. I could no longer rest until their safety and their message was protected. I reasoned that if, like Christ himself, they were truly sent to earth by divine intentions, then no effort to protect them was too much.

Whether we realize it or not, humankind is standing on the edge. The White Lions herald coming changes on this earth, just as Christ himself spoke of these changes. At the end of days, Christ says, 'the sun will be darkened and the moon will not give its light, the stars will fall from the sky and the heavenly bodies will be shaken. At this prophetic time, events on earth will be quite clearly manifest in the heavens. Christ tells us, 'At that time, the sign of the son of man will appear in the sky.'

For me, the death of Ingwavuma signaled the death of a kingdom on earth, with ominous resonances of Christ's prophetic words about signs in the sky preceding the end of the world. Earth tremors [like that in Turkey, and more recently in India and Ecuador] are early warning signal that, although we might believe otherwise, we are not lords of the planet. We might believe we can breed the Sun God's hallowed children as stuffed trophies. We might believe we can mess with genetics. In these beliefs, I believe we are profoundly misguided. We cannot master nature, nature is one with God the Master.

... I am doing everything I can to protect Aslan and Tendile and other [white lions] of their kind from the hunter's bullet. As the lion ancestors have taught me, I am a Lionness of God, or at least I try to be. Before I take any step, even before I commit any word to paper, I ask for guidance from God that the steps I am taking and the words I am uttering are in accordance with his Great Will and His Great Plan ... as a woman who feels personally wounded by the killing of Ingwama, I am sometimes overcome with tremendous anger: in respect to the wealthy American who killed Ingwama for a trophy, I know who he is, and I wonder what deep psychological problem led this individual to commit such an act. His decision to kill a lion was obviously a conscious one, but made without consciousness, without conscience. I believe this individual will carry the blood of my lion on his soul, whether he knows it or not.

The White Lion message, nature's message, is unfolding at this very moment.

I do not believe it is too late. We all know what is needed. We need to protect the White Lions, just as we need to protect all forms of life on our planet. We need to stop all forms of damage to our planet. We need to start seeing the signs being shown to us in each and every aspect of our natural world. We need to stop seeing life exclusively in terms of money, when material values and spiritual values are ultimately one and the same thing. We need to start taking responsibilities for the state of our earth. We need to stop walking blindly, like sleepwalkers, into our own-created doom. We need to stand still for a moment—and start waking up.

Our route toward spiritual evolution is radiantly clear. We all have our own unique individual journey to walk toward enlightenment. Living on the brink of evolutionary change means that new grounds are being broken, new consciousness is being raised. Truth is of the essence—we have no dogma, no set formulae, no prescribed rules, no false standards to follow. All we have is the truth within our souls. I believe most people want to follow the light, the path of healing and not destroying our earth, but we don't have the courage, the *'lion-heart'* [my italic], to follow our individual truth toward enlightenment. Giving in to our fears, we bury our 'gold' beneath the false systems of our societies, and we attempt to comfort ourselves with the notion that we have no power or responsibility for what is happening in the world.

If we overcome our fears, I believe we all have the power of light—the White Lion. To have 'white light' is to be enlightened. To be enlightened is to work not only with right thoughts but with right actions. And to work with principles of light in thoughts, words and actions is to be empowered to make a difference for good on earth. This is our challenge. This is what I believe God's White Lions are asking of us at this critical time in humankind's evolutionary history.

Until we realign ourselves with the forces of light, of sunlight, of light-energy that breathes the very word 'life' to each and every life form on this planet, we are aligning ourselves with darkness. Until we reinstate, within our own lives, the sacred geometry and divine principles of balance and harmony in accordance with the natural laws of the sun—the solar logos—we are inevitably heading to plunge ourselves into appalling upheaval and chaos. The cosmic laws of our universe are meaningful and profoundly logical; it is we humans, rather, who have lost our divine logic.

In the dark and challenging days that lie ahead, there are two truths we should never forget in our quest for golden enlightenment. The lion is the symbol of the soul essence of humankind. And the soul is eternal ...[66]

The Elders, the few that are left in the various Indian tribes, are still listening. Are we? The White Buffalo *is* the representative on our Northern Continent, on this side of the Earth, and like their brothers in Africa they are sending their Message, coming to the earth at the same time. That is not a coincidence. And it's all the more reason to be living on a farm and taking care of the earth.

More troubles have come our way. Our mare, eight-year-old China, has cut her front left foot. She cut the artery and the ligament, all the way into the joint. It happened in the evening when she ran through, or on top of, a sheet of aluminum while the door to the barn was being fixed and the

66. Linda Tucker, *The Mystery of the White Lions* (Mapumulanga, S.A.: Npenvu Press, 2003), pp. 342–345.

yard had not been thoroughly cleaned up. She came home from the veterinary hospital with a cast on her foot. For now, we can be thankful that there is no infection, but we do not know if she will be able to walk correctly. We are all very upset because she is such a beautiful animal, extremely intelligent, kind, and good on the trails. I go and visit her throughout the day to see how she is. She is very patient. The other horses watch her, wondering what has happened.

❧

I have been in the kitchen for days now and I am finished with plum and peach jams and tomato sauce. Everything is neatly put away for the winter, and the smell of fall is in the air. More rain has fallen in the already-soaked fields, and now several farms are unable to harvest. There will be much loss. Many farms north of us, and in the west as well, have had to dump their milk, because the roads are inaccessible for the big milk trucks. The same is true for the vegetable harvest; it is too muddy to get into the fields. It is sunny today, however, and the earth will dry.

The big fair has begun and I spend my first day there watching the workhorses perform. It is one of my favorite events of the fair. Enormous Clydesdales pull colorful wagons in teams of two, four, six, or eight. There are divisions for men, women, and juniors driving these teams of flamboyant horses. All—men, women, and horses—are in their finest attire. The owners have spent the last week preparing for this fair. I love to go into the big barn and watch the frantic activities of whole families as they get these enormous animals ready. Grandpa is doing one last check on

The canning is finished and ready for storage

the woven tail; young girls are shining the silver equipment; the wife is cleaning the stalls; the husband is putting on his western outfit. Everything is ready for the entrance into the arena and excitement is high. I take a lot of pictures because the scene is so beautiful, and it speaks of a past long gone!

There are only a few participants in these shows throughout the country, especially in the Midwest, where people do not have much money but they make do. It shows in their love for their horses. It is their life. We sit and enjoy the show, but we should actually pay these people to maintain this art of working with horses. They do it because they love it, and when this work stops, we will lose a great deal.

In their barn, these docile giants look gently at the visitors. They will remain on the grounds for the next four days in their small stalls. I also love to look at the trucks which are used to transport them from their farms, enormous trucks with trailers converted for the huge beasts. I always enjoy watching them depart, journeying down the road with their heavy precious loads. There are many women who handle the great animals, and most of the time they are tiny women—wearing gloves.

The judges have a hard time deciding the winners. Participants should receive a check just for showing up, because they actually get nothing for coming to show us their magnificent animals. They are only here because of their love of workhorses. And nowadays that is very rare and special.

Everyone comes to the fair. All the old folks meet friends and neighbors; often these farmers came to this country generations ago from Germany, Holland, Sweden, Norway, Switzerland, or Denmark. They have all mingled, worked hard on the farms, and made this country what it is. They still work hard, but now they are faced with a multitude of problems. Because they are eating foods that are poisoned by pesticides and other chemicals, their health is deteriorating. This year more than other years I have seen far, far more elderly people in wheelchairs with oxygen tanks at their sides. Some look as if they have had a stroke, or they are too obese to walk anymore. I estimate the average size of most of the people at the fair is at least 50 pounds overweight. The younger children are getting overweight as well, and until the large food companies who sell garbage start having a conscience, the U.S. is in for troubles. The fairgrounds offered nothing but junk food, and everyone I saw was eating hotdogs laced with poisonous substances, corn dogs, hamburgers, artificially colored sugar candy, french fries, ice cream, white rolls and bread, or potatoes filled with fat cheese. The country is poisoning its workforce, its children, and its old people and no one is doing anything about it. People buy poisoned milk, poisoned vegetables, fruits, meats, corn chips, potato chips, sodas, and beer and do not realize that what they put inside their stomach will cause heart attacks and put them in wheel chairs. It is devastating to watch, especially when I go to the children's dairy barn, steer, or sheep barns. These children are in our care; they have no idea what is good or bad. We give them our habits, our ways of cooking and eating. We guide their lifestyle.

In the barns, these youngsters are working seriously with their pet cows, cleaning them up so they can look the best. They wash their feet and their tails, brush their coats so they shine, clean the stalls so the cows are immaculate, bring them water in pails, feed them hay, and clean up the manure. One little boy was fast asleep in his sleeping bag against his little calf that he had cleaned. A two-year-old was sweeping the floor with a broom bigger than he was. A lanky teenage young man was sleeping on an old sofa, exhausted from having gotten up at 3:00 a.m. to milk the cows at home before bringing some of them here to the fair. Young girls clean the little pigs that sleep soundly in their pig pen waiting for us visitors to look at their beautiful pinkness. The goats are shiny and the sheep have had their hair cut, and some girls are doing last-minute hair trimming on their beautiful sheep, making them ready for the show ring.

At this fair the American spirit is still present and alive, but it is being assaulted by a food industry that is not concerned about what is good for the human being, and the hardworking farmers are the first ones to suffer. They need to wake up and go back to eating fresh food grown on unspoiled lands and drink sweet water or cider from fresh apples rather than consuming corn dogs and sodas.

❧

There is much sadness in our little community today. Our singing teacher, Mary, has left this world to enter the next one, leaving her husband and two darling little ones. She brought much music to all our community meetings over the last ten years. I am especially grateful for my daughter's singing in her Waldorf school, because my daughter sang her way through her childhood years. I called my daughter to tell her and she lit lots of candles in the big cathedral in Barcelona, in remembrance of her teacher who brought the children songs from all over the world. I spent some time saying some prayers and reading with Mary during the three-day vigil at her home, and felt her presence there very strongly, as everyone else did. She looked like Sleeping Beauty. How appropriate that she died on the month of the virgin, the Sophia month, and there she will deposit all of her wonderful songs and strength of spirit. The angel world will be very happy to receive such a rich and joyful soul, and we will miss her greatly here at our community gatherings, her clear voice and crystal-clear blue eyes.

Hundreds of people came to say good-bye, and the Community Priest was deeply in touch with Mary's soul and spirit. We were all very fortunate to be there. Mary allowed a huge opening into the spirit world for all of us, an enormous bridge. We all thanked her. It was a beautiful early fall day, with not a cloud in the sky, and everyone went home with a deepened soul. A courageous soul had gone to eternal life to meet her maker.

I went back to the fair and took the two little ones with me, and we watched the cowgirls and cowboys ride and compete in several games. Back at the farm, we had a breakfast the day after the funeral for the children, their dad, family, and friends to say a final good-bye. We quietly contemplated the large Pieta which I had just finished painting last week, and then we all went to the local lake for a swim. The water was refreshing after the last few intense days.

Now it is afternoon, the rooster sings, the hummingbirds drink nectar at a feverish pace before their long trip south, the sparrows feed their young who are now as big as they are, the tall cranes hang around the distant meadow and make their magic sound, and the last batches of chicks, six of them, are just born. The tomatoes are harvested. The apples fall on the ground and the horses are happy to eat them. The zinnias are at their best, and it is time to collect some flower seeds for next year.

Beautiful fall weather is here again, and the horses are up to mischief. The stallion somehow took down a huge iron fence separating him from his mother China, the injured horse, and now they are both walking around the meadows. How he did it is a mystery. The partition fence is made of metal bars, and the horse had to drag the door-fence outside past the heavy Bobcat, and drag it over the fence outside. That stallion is definitely extremely intelligent. Again, I cannot deal with horse problems, but need to wait until their master comes home. And I am alone with the horses for another two weeks. There is never a dull moment here. If the horse could move that door, then he can get out of anywhere, and I am a bit worried about that.

The vet came and said China's walking is doing better and that perhaps she will fully recover. The stallion is back with his friend Silky, and Max has still not found a new home. Arian, the German shepherd, is roaming, the chickens are running around before their long winter in their condo-chicken coop, the cows are eating as always, and the sheep are happy that the days are getting colder. The bees have an enormous amount of honey stored, and all is ready in their hives for their winter sleep. I have finished all my jobs, the barn has been cleaned, and hay is in the barn. Now I can plan some more travels.

The fall is here, the nights are getting cooler, and this weekend was the official end of summer. Our little town celebrates every year with a "band scramble." It starts on Friday night when the organizers decorate the town square and serve corn on the cob, bratwursts, and beer. The next day bluegrass bands come from the whole surrounding area for a competition, and musicians from 5 years old to 80 or older come to show their skills and compete in various musical categories. They play banjo, violin, guitar, fiddle, and bass, or sing bluegrass. Here is what I love about this little town: at this festival the young still mingle with the old, the old are teaching the young music, and there is no wall between the generations, only a wonderful sharing of music. Families play music together, music which originated in the U.S. with influences coming from the old country, especially Ireland, uniting African blues, gospel music, and fiddle. It is truly American music, the best this country has to offer. The old-timers come from barns, farms, shops, factories, and Wal-Mart jobs, and participate in the forever-young playing of music. The whole square wakes up for a few days, as the whole town shows up with their folding chairs or blankets to listen to this upbeat, wonderfully rhythmic music from the olden days.

The famous bands which are hired by the sponsors arrive in enormous tour buses from North Carolina, Kentucky, Louisiana, and of course all over Wisconsin. They play continuously for two days in various corners of the square and have jam sessions of their own while other bands are playing on the stage. Only acoustic instruments are allowed, and pieces are played from memory. Men and women participate, although there are more men than women. I even thought of getting myself a huge bass. It only has a few strings and I like the sound. If I do that I will definitely have become an American.

It is a joy to see that all is not dead around here; music is the language for the weekend. Many of the musicians play songs with Christian themes, gospels songs, and love ballads, as well as songs lamenting life's sorrows. It makes me think of troubadours of old, alive and well in this part of the Midwest. Seeing the old men still youthful and playing their seasoned instruments reminds me that all is not lost, and there is still some soul left even though the soul has been attacked from all quarters. These musicians play all year long in garages, basements, churches, and living rooms, four or five of them together keeping something alive. The grandchildren step up on the stage following their grandfathers or grandmothers and, in turn, play tunes of ages past on their child-sized instruments. There is a warm brotherhood extending throughout the whole town. People meet friends they have not seen for the whole year, and then it is good-bye and everyone goes home with more warmth in their hearts, ready for another year of cold wintry days, ice storms, blizzards, and high winds, until the next fall. And so, on that note I will end this year's Wisconsin hills farms stories until next spring.

❧

Spring is here! We have had a long winter with record-breaking snowfall. The town square still has a pile of snow, and it is mid-April. The chickens are out foraging happily on the farm grounds. We cleaned up their home and it is sparkling with clean straw left over from our oat planting of several years ago. The mother hen is hovering over her four little chicks, one black, one light yellow, and two others of various shades that blend with the outside world.

Now we have the headache of selling the eggs, which are plentiful—at least twenty eggs, more or less, each day—much more than we need. We are not "real" farmers, meaning our income is derived from other professions. So I have to go with my basket to friends to sell these eggs. I spend an average of $1200 a year on organic feed from western Wisconsin to keep this flock of about 34 chickens healthy. I sell the eggs at $4.00 a dozen, and most people will not buy my eggs at that price. It actually costs me about $10 a dozen if I were to include the labor of cleaning, feeding, and watering the chickens. How do farmers live in order to feed the world if they cannot feed themselves with the proceeds of their work? Here it costs just as much to buy a dozen eggs as to buy a plastic bottle of distilled water or a bottle of soda.

Since I spend most of my time doing cultural work such as painting, teaching, healing, and scholarly work, being on the farm keeps me in touch with the reality of everyday life. I can paint paintings all day, but I have eight dozen eggs, beautifully colored, healthy eggs, sitting on my counter and no one to buy them unless I drive around, call people, and sometimes plead, "Unless you people buy my eggs, I must turn my chickens into food, which I deplore doing. I absolutely hate to kill these wonderful, happy chickens and eat them when I can feed myself very well just with their eggs." People do not realize that supporting the farmer-food provider is their job. The farmer's job is to grow the food as best he or she can. I go through this every spring. My husband is more practical and says that we only need five chickens for ourselves. He asks why I want all these chickens. My thinking was, if I can provide others with good food, why not? It is not much more work dealing with thirty chickens. But the people who should be thankful for this work do not care.

It is the same problem everywhere. Here I deal with it in the most ordinary way: selling eggs. Should I spend my time running around trying to sell a few eggs or paint in my studio? I cannot do everything. We do not have a co-op here.

Then I plunged into Rudolf Steiner's work on the threefold social order and glimpsed the answers. My work as an artist, which belongs to the cultural, religious domain, belongs to the individual. My work on the farm, which provides goods for individuals, belongs to the economic sphere. And here Steiner states that one cannot do anything as an individual, which is clearly evident by my complaints. I can drive around as much as I want, and make phone calls to all my friends, but it will not help me sell my eggs. Here Steiner states that we must form organizations which deal with other organizations.

> ... The human being must grasp science on his own; religion he must generate for himself; art he must bring forth from the wellspring of his individual being, the innermost fountain of his personality. These must proceed from the most wide awake,

clearest consciousness. Here, he must rely entirely upon himself, upon his individuality ...[67]

... Where man as an individual confronts mankind as a whole, it is necessary to form associations; it is necessary that judgments or decisions be formulated by individuals in associations, hence, that individuals pool their experiences. Deeds and accomplishments then must spring from associations, not from individual personalities. Here we are referred to a life where the individual person can do nothing by himself, where he can accomplish something only when he is part of an association, and where the association enters into reciprocal relationships with another association. In short, we are directed to what really takes place within the human social community in this duller consciousness—the economic sphere of the social organism.[68]

In the summer months, I do belong to a co-op where I buy a share of vegetables. This is becoming very popular. We pay for four months of vegetables in order to help the farmers live. I miss the farm initiative we belonged to in New Hampshire that I wrote about earlier, but that group was ahead of the times. The Eastern part of the U.S. is much more awakened than the sleepy Midwest. What is missing here is a group of individuals having the same vision, and dedication to such a venture. Here, many of us own a farm but nothing is accomplished in the way of working together.

67. Rudolf Steiner, *Spiritual Science as a Foundation for Social Forms*, Lecture in Dornach September 4, 1920 (Great Barrington, MA: SteinerBooks, 1986), p. 213.

68. Ibid., p. 214.

I tried to plant the seeds of such thinking but was told repeatedly that here in the Midwest we work each in our own way. We looked for a way to form what we had in New Hampshire, but no one wanted to share their land, or even sell an acre of land so that we could pull our resources together for buying tractors, equipment, and so on. The result is, we bought our own farm and had to buy old equipment—everything is at least 50 years old on the farm—which my maverick son and husband know how to fix and enjoy fixing.

I have seen many farmers come here in the last 12 years and repeat the same errors—buying equipment, falling into debt, and being unable to continue farming. No associations are formed to help the farmers; they are all working as individuals. They need to be supported by a group of people who will buy their products. We are still waiting.

The farmers complain constantly whenever we have a conversation, and it is always the same: "We do not get paid for our services." Yet, when one mentions, "Well why not have a meeting of people once a year, and ask them to pay in advance for the services?" the answer is, "Oh no, that would never work!" So it goes, and nothing can be achieved. As Steiner notes so clearly, when dealing with the economic sphere, one must form associations. Until that day comes, I can grow all I want but it will reach few. Farmers can scream all they want, but unless they form an association with other farmers and associations with buyers, nothing will come of it except more complaints and hard feelings between farmers and customers.

Therefore, concerning my eggs, I am going to have a "chicken-eggs production supported by friends," and they will have to pay for one year and receive two dozen eggs per week for the price of $320. That is one beginning. In this

I am not an artist; I just take care of my chickens, so they are happy sitting and making healthy eggs. If my friends do not want to support this "chicken-eggs" operation, then my chickens will be given away. There will be no more nice eggs, unless they take responsibility and buy the eggs as a group.

My work as an artist, which is in the sphere of Culture/Art and not the Economic sphere, is where I only deal with myself and my work with paint, and the substances of the earth have interfered with my work as a farmer-gardener. Not until I realized what Steiner meant by associations when dealing with economics did it sink in. Although I did belong to associations, they were from the customer's perspective, not from my stand as a farmer producing eggs. Every spring the same nonsense goes on.

> ... Because the economic sphere acts upon the astral body [feeling body], brotherliness that should exist in the economic sphere is borne through the portal of death, for the human being takes along his astral body for a certain time. What is thus established by virtue of brotherliness in the human soul is carried through death into the spiritual world, and there continues to be effective as such....[69]

This makes sense. Because I care about the person who is providing me with milk, I buy his product for the right amount so that he does not starve, and a spirit of brotherhood comes into being between the consumer and the producer through association. My friends care about my producing good eggs, therefore they pay for them ahead of time. Well, enough about my eggs.

---

69. Ibid., pp. 221–222.

🌿

The wind is blowing from the southeast, announcing unsettling weather. It is blowing strongly over the entire Midwest, moving large clouds. One day heavy fog and cold rain, the next blue skies, and so on. Nothing is stable in the spring here. My orchard hopefully will be safe from a very cold, freezing night which could destroy all the young buds, meaning no fruits like last year. All the blossoms were frozen, and there were no peaches.

And here we see that this weather pattern, huge clouds blowing across continents, do not come from nowhere!

... The course taken by wind and weather today, hence the manner in which the rhythm of our external climate develops, is essentially the continuation of rhythms brought about by the life of rights in the social organism of past ages.

The human being stands indeed in a certain relationship to outer reality, even the reality of nature. It is important to realize that what develops all around us as the sphere of rights is not something merely abstract, man-made, arising and again disappearing; instead, what is at first a thought content, having its being initially in the realm of rights [law], lives in a subsequent age of earth existence in the atmosphere, in the vibrations, in the entire configuration, and in the movements of the atmosphere.

... We have a certain kind of weather, wind and so forth, seasons with this or that configuration. Now we experience externally, in the atmosphere, what once upon a time we set up as the order of justice....

... What at one time is a social system of rights conceived by the mind will become an order of nature at another, albeit distant, future time. With the help of spiritual science one can see how the thought-out political order of one age is connected with the atmospheric order of nature of another time....[70]

We live in this world. Because of the way and manner in which we have been placed into the social context of the world, we have a certain state of mind. We confront those with whom we come into contact in life with certain rights' concepts or concepts and sensations resembling the feelings of rights. This gives our soul a certain configuration. Simply speaking, let us say that I have a certain relationship to ten people in life. The one I love, the other I hate, I am indifferent to the third, I am dependent on the fourth, the fifth is dependent on me, and so on. In the most diverse ways, then, my rights and duties concerning these ten persons are outlined. All this crystallizes into a certain soul state in me, but not only in a superficial manner, for the emotional fiber of my soul is conditioned by it. This position within the social order from the viewpoint of the rights sphere brings about a certain configuration of my etheric [body], which is transmitted to the cosmos upon my death. After this body separates from me, what vibrates in my

---

70. Ibid., pp. 219–221.

etheric body here [on earth] continues to vibrate in the cosmos, causing further reverberations.[71]

Considering what is going on in the world in the sphere of rights, we are in deep trouble for the future. The rights of individuals are forever being taken away, to be replaced by the rights of the state, to instill fear and domination. What global companies do to the earth when they ignore or deny the rights of human beings, but honor the right to make lots of money, leads everyone to become slaves with no rights. We are going to suffer enormous cataclysms. We are already being confronted with incredible forces of nature gone wild, and they are bound to become wilder. All the scientists studying nature and the weather, however, have not the foggiest idea that when people have no rights and are enslaved by others, this forms the weather of the future. It's myopic thinking at its best. Rudolf Steiner did the best he could to bring clarity into this very complicated matter, but few are aware.

> ... In order to render rescue possible, it is necessary that a sufficiently large number of people rouse themselves inwardly. For, particularly in the present epoch, the possibility exists in man's inner being to pick up those threads of a soul-spiritual kind which, if their power is inwardly experienced in the proper way, lead to an understanding of what can be gathered from spiritual science for an illumination of the life of nature as well as the social life. One should not wish to retain at all costs the bad habits of one's inner life, however they have developed during the

---

71. Ibid., pp. 218–219.

past few centuries. These bad habits are based on the opinion that if one can keep quiet and be passive, the gods will eventually enter into one, reveal everything within, and mystical depth will be illumined by an inner light, and so forth. The present age is not suited for that. It demands an inner activity of soul and spirit from the human being; it demands that man turn and look at what is trying to reveal itself within. Then, he will find under all circumstances what wishes to reveal itself within, but he must be willing to unfold such inner spiritual activity. One must not believe, however, that much can be gained by some inner pseudomystical doings; above all else, one has to trace the spirit in the external things of the world.[72]

Our mare, China, who was injured, is doing very well, galloping in the meadows and only showing a slight limp when walking—a miracle. I still hope that she can be ridden some day. The young stallion is now a gelding, and he is also doing well. He acts more like a dog than a horse. He comes to be petted, or just to be around us. He now is led around as a pack horse, and in a couple of months he will be ridden for the first time. One of the Angus cows has delivered, and I am worried about another pregnant cow which is quite small. I hope she will not have problems delivering her calf, and I need to watch her every day. The sheep each have two lambs. We only lost one lamb when the mother refused to feed him, and he died during the night when the weather was 20 degrees below zero.

---

72. Ibid., 249-250.

Feeding the lambs

This year it seems that spring is quite late; the grass is hardly growing. The bees have woken up, and they have survived, so we are relieved. The pond garden needs to be cleaned out, and this year our fish died for the first time in years. So this morning I woke up early to face this huge task. The lotus plants have taken over the pond, and the mud is more than a foot deep. It all has to be removed by hand, and my husband refused to help because he says the pond is mine. I agreed.

I empty it with a pump, and then climb inside it and take the mud out by the bucketful. I am swimming in muck, with tadpoles all around me and mud on my face, hair, and clothes. I take out all the enormous healthy lotus roots and put them elsewhere, just keeping a few plants. Then I wash the sides of the pond, take out all the rocks, and rinse the muck underneath. Little by little, after a few hours, crystal clean water

The water garden next to the farmhouse

flows into the clean pond. It is worth the hard work watching the little stream which flows into the pond right by the house with the lilies, irises, and other plants. It is a place for relaxing and watching the birds use it as a gigantic birth bath.

❧

This Sunday I watched a movie about the huge corporations, which sell chemicals to the world and produce Frankenstein plants. It was extremely painful to watch this documentary about the degeneration of our planet. Now the seeds are being taken over by the powers of selfishness, which want to make all the farmers slaves to the seed corporations. Friends here are doing research on corn and finding that corn hybrids are contaminating all the organic corn. Seed savers are active, but nothing can really stop this technology of inserting DNA material into the cells of the plants, or anything else for that matter.

From studying lectures on the threefold social order—the spiritual-religious-artistic sphere, the rights sphere, and the economic sphere—it is clear that we are here only in one sphere, and that it is the economic sphere that is taking over the government as well as the religious sphere. Watching this movie I could clearly see the economic sphere invading the religious sphere and the damage it is causing. The scientist in his lab, injecting matter into a cell and designing a new plant, is playing god in a way only based on money. The practical outcome of selling more seeds forbids the farmer from collecting seeds, as they "belong" to the company. Thereby, the life of the plants belongs to the company that is making money. The demarcation between life and economy is no longer. The economic sphere owns the life sphere, the spiritual sphere.

Rudolf Steiner points out that the economic sphere is related to the human etheric body, and I feel that the mingling of the economic sphere with the sphere of life, the ether body, is a sign that something is wrong. When decisions about the economic spheres are made by certain individuals who are extremely and insatiably greedy, the decisions are not made by a group of people united in brotherhood, leading to our present situation. Steiner's warnings have fallen on deaf ears.

❧

The Midwest Horse Fair is happening this weekend in Madison, and I will attend the three full days of "horsing around." The event centers around the Department of Wildlife, an organization which takes care of the wild mustangs that roam freely in some Western states, such as Arizona, Colorado, Nevada, and Wyoming. They have given 50 of them to trainers who have worked 100 days with these wild horses that have never seen human beings, since they came directly from the wild. The trainers are bringing their horses from all over the country to demonstrate what they have achieved with them during the hundred days. Among the 50,000 or so people who come to the fair, there is great anticipation about this event.

Driving to the fair early on this cold morning, I can see the many farms scattered across this prairie land. Miles and miles of corn and soybeans will be planted here in the next few weeks, and in the distance I can see the large silos full of corn and the newly built generator to burn the corn and extract ethanol for use as fuel. The mathematics of this venture are staggering. It costs far more to grow the corn than the financial benefit of the ethanol. The farmers' subsidies will allow the farmer to waste whole fields of corn that will be fed to the Ethanol plant rather than to the cows. The result of such nonsensical thinking is that people in far-away lands will grow hungry because the farmer would rather produce ethanol with the government's help than allow the corn to be fed to people in developing countries who cannot pay as much for corn as food as the farmer makes for corn as fuel.

Driving around the Midwest makes me angry this morning, and it is not even 7:00 a.m. It is an hour and a half drive to get to Madison, and I see at least four new large ethanol plants that were not there last year. These plants cost a lot, and one wonders where that money comes from. Another result of the ethanol industry is that the farmers will not be growing soybeans, but corn, and probably not hay for animals either. So the result will be less hay for our horses and cows and sheep, and few will likely grow wheat and oats. We see the result of that kind of thinking here in the U.S. with our increasing food prices. People are beginning to buy large amounts of staples, hoarding because they are afraid that they will starve, and it begins a spiral of panic.

The entrance to the fair is very busy with incoming traffic and I finally park the car and walk among the throng of horse lovers. These people have driven from miles around, some from nearby states—Iowa, Minnesota, Kansas, Indiana, Illinois, Michigan, Wisconsin—and others with their mustangs from as far away as Maine or Texas, all at their own expense.

There are horse trailers everywhere and excitement is in the air. There are many clinics throughout the arenas, under tents, inside the dome, and in small enclosures where horse trainers share their techniques. I run from one to another, connecting with some people and not with others. I want to see all the mustang trainers and compare their ways of working, so I spend a great deal of time watching them. They come in all shapes and ages, from young college girls and cattle ranch hands, to 75-year-old horse lovers and middle-aged men and women. I stay glued to my seat, not wanting to miss out on even one of the trainers. I learn more about their personalities than I do about their horses. With some trainers, they are all about themselves, not about the horses, and they tend to be bossy and showy. I notice they are not so fluid, but calcified in their actions, even harsh, and the horses respond nervously. With some young female trainers there is pure love between the large animals and themselves, and their action is more fluid, not about large selfish egos, but rather selfless egos. Their horses feel at ease and do as they are told. The whole experience is living psychology. For some older men and women, it seems to be pure fun inter-acting with the animals, and they are obviously gifted in their abilities. With some it is nothing but pure "me." You can see it in the way they walk around. Those people get on my nerves, and I am repulsed by what they are doing, even though they might be quite good at their work.

I hardly eat or drink, but enjoy getting lost in what is happening between the horse and rider. It is totally fascinat-ing, and I think it must be one of the few activities left to modern men and women in which the individual can work with such incredible raw power. I myself have a hard time telling such a huge animal what to do, but I feel that deep inside if I am truly myself, the horse will pick up on what I want, so I will not need to give orders.

In the evening I buy a ticket to the rodeo, which I have never seen in person. I did see a "corrida" or "bullfight" in Barcelona 35 years ago and was disgusted with the violence and swore I would never go again. The rodeo coliseum-arena is large and packed with spectators, and I sit right over the area where the men are mounting the wild broncos and bulls. It is again mesmerizing to see these wild-crazy men take on such dangerous work. I observe that before they tie them-selves to the horse or bull, they sit quietly, totally absorbed in themselves, as if in a recollection or meditation, and most of them kiss their cross or Mary Medal and cross themselves in the custom of the Catholic Church. Trusting in destiny is a marvelous act of belief and humility. These men cannot go in the ring without that act of trust in a higher being, and that is touching. The wilder they look the more humble and devout they seem. My seat is very close and high, and I can see everything very clearly without being seen myself. In these moments these riders pause in utter loneliness—just them and their faith in a higher power, at peace in the face of death or great injury.

Then they ride the wildest horses I have ever seen, horses that are irritated by having a rope tied around their middle, something they obviously cannot stand. I feel back in time, perhaps watching Roman gladiators. It is a horror to see men thrown in the air as if they are rag dolls and then fall to the ground with a dead noise, some unable to get up. They are helped, obviously hurting. I feel guilty that my money has perpetuated such acts of cruelty. Then the bull comes. By now my hair is standing on end! A man ties his hand to a rope tied to an enormous bulls with horns. This huge animal jumps in the air as if he is a ballerina, the rider falls off, risking being trampled by the full power of the bull's 1800 pounds or more, and is taken out on a stretcher with multiple injuries. The next rider is tied to the next bull for the next ride, and he too makes the sign of the cross and goes to his fate. The entrance fees—my money included—is given to the winner. I swear this day that I will never again watch such acts of cruelty and violence.

The horses which are used to helping the rodeo riders dismount the wild broncos or bulls are amazing. I have never seen such exceptional horsemanship and art between rider and horses. In a breathtaking series of events, they run at a full gallop trying to untie the one who is sitting on top of a wild bull or horse. They must ride right up against the arena walls close to the bull, reach out to get the rider, pick him up and sit him on their own mount while the wild horse or bull goes on. The ability of the two horsemen means the difference between a man dying or not. It is too much for me, and probably for the other spectators as well. Where else does one see death except in battle during war? Here in the Midwest we set it up so that we can see death and injury for our enjoyment. By the end of the evening, I am beside myself over how barbaric we all are, including me for sitting through the entire performance. I made myself stay, but will never do so again. Driving home in the rain, I am exhausted by the events of the day.

I sleep dreaming of horses and get up very early the next day for an encore after feeding my own animals at 6:00 a.m. Again the day begins with the fifty trainers, coming this time into the huge arena for six- to seven-minute demonstrations of what they have accomplished with their animals. All day, horses and trainers enter the arena showing off their skills. What is most beautiful to watch is the range of skills which the trainers have transferred to their horses. The young girls simply ride English wearing beautiful matching outfits of white riding pants and black jacket, and in some cases do jumps. The cowboy maneuvers his horse in intense shapes to rope an invisible calf, comes to an abrupt stop by the fence, and throws ropes around the horse's neck. There is a dressage horse showing off his ability to dance, doing fancy footsteps at the slight signal from the rider. An old cowboy rides with his best friend and in the end stands on the top of the saddle, only to fall off because of a slight movement of the horse—the rider's fault. One horse does the trick of bowing to the audience while standing on a small wooden stand. Everyone is mesmerized by these incredible men and women with their mustangs that had been wild just three months earlier. The horses are geldings and mares that are more than three or four years old. They come in all colors—17 hands high, majestic and alert or 13 hands small, witty and energetic.

Some of the cowboys ride swiftly across the arena and end their routine by firing a gun from the horse. The horse calmly does as he is told. We are all wildly impressed by one most majestic being who can imitate her master-rider with utmost, selfless imitation. In most cases total trust has developed between the horse and rider.

During the break I go to chat with some of the riders, and am very surprised to learn that most of them do not ride professionally, and that they sometimes only have time to work with the mustangs an hour or less in the evening after having worked at their jobs all day. One trainer we happen to know lives half an hour from our farm and has trained his horse to be an entertainment act. His horse, called Elvis, is a beautiful black, shiny, muscular horse. The trainer, who is Mexican with Indian blood, dresses up in his finest show clothes and uses a saddle decorated with silver, so the whole arena is totally captivated. Horse and rider come into the arena as if they own it, and the crowd loves the incredible bond between them and their ability to entertain us with pirouettes, jumping, chasing an invisible calf, bowing to the audience, and dancing. At the end of his 6-7 minutes, he takes off the bridle and the reins and rides the horse using just a small rope around the horse's neck, only giving cues with his legs. It seems that he merely thinks a turn and the horse obeys. The crowd goes wild. On the final day on Sunday when all the horses go up for auction, his horse fetches $10,000, the most paid for a horse at the fair. No one would have guessed that this horse had been roaming in the wilds of northern Nevada just three months earlier. This type of showmanship is new at the horse fair and it is taking off like wild fire. This summer, Texas will host its own mustang contest with 200 horses and riders; I will perhaps go to watch.

During the fair I sign up for a weekend with one of the very successful presenters, a woman from California. She loves her horses and is in the process of starting a brand new Las Vegas act with the horses as the main attraction. Among the horses she brought to Madison is a black one that her husband rides that was supposed to be put to sleep, but they rescued him and worked with him over several years using new methods. Their other horse, a white one, is famous because he was in a movie. She bought this beautiful horse from his original trainer and now does all sorts of tricks with him. Her training uses love, rhythm, consistency and "horse language." I buy the videos of this method so that I can use it myself with my own horses to face up to my fears.

One can see that the horses are her children. She lives for her animals, and they drive across the country in huge trailers with their horses inside. I can travel alone anywhere in the world among all sorts of people with no problem, but driving a trailer with horses inside is something that I wish I could do, but cannot. Many of my friends are comfortable doing it, and truck their horses an hour away several times a week to ride in the state park. Perhaps my fear comes from other lifetimes in which I might have been injured or died as a result of riding. I do not know, but it is deep-seated, and I work on it constantly when I ride. When I was younger I did not have this fear and rode whenever I got a chance; this fear has come surreptitiously as I have gotten older. But perhaps I am being practical, and just cannot take a chance on falling off and breaking anything, since I love to walk more than I love to ride. One must make choices, sometimes hard ones. But I do not give up.

❧

I drive to a small town in southern Wisconsin on a beautiful day, taking small roads to get to the place where the horse-training weekend is taking place. I arrive a bit late and the presentation has already started. There are 25-30 people of all ages there and our lady presenter and her husband are there to teach us tirelessly about their new way of handling horses—with love. She shows us how to greet the horse before doing anything, by having him smell the hand, which is like asking permission to meet the horse. The smelling of the hand means that the horse knows you, and greets you. Then you pat him on the forehead. The trainer wants us to bring a chair inside our own arena at home in a meadow and just sit there with a book, while the horse runs around. We need to let the horse observe us and come to us, and then little by little with several other rituals, the horse will follow us around like a dog would. It is simply magic to observe all this, and I am glad that I bought the whole series of DVDs so that I can spend more time using these methods.

We all enjoy the two-day retreat with these two very special people and their beloved animals. The warmth exhibited in the arena between all the people from all walks of life is a pleasure to feel. A woman in her early thirties sits next to me, a no-nonsense tall attractive lady who tells me she has five horses. I ask her what she does for a living and she says she is a policewoman and works in a town that I go to several times in the summer called Spring Green. It is the home of an outdoor Shakespearean theater which I love. I tell her that perhaps I will meet her on the road, as I often drive too fast!

At the end of the presentation, people bring their problem horses and that is even more informative. The problems of the riders themselves show in the horse they are working with. It is so apparent that it surprises me greatly to observe their dramas played out through their animals. There is a girl who had stopped working with the horse who had been her companion on many adventures. He had been her faithful comrade for showing and jumping, and then she gave the horse to her mother and got herself another horse, which she needed for further work. She literally abandoned her companion when he was no longer of any use to her. Watching the horse in the arena, we can tell he has something wrong with him. He looks like he is thoroughly disgusted, not interested in life at all. He only stands and reluctantly does a few things when asked. He is a severely depressed horse. The trainer, of course, grasps the situation right away and tells the young woman that what she has done is wrong: "You abandoned this horse after spending years with him in the show ring, and you just let him go when he was no longer useful? What kind of behavior is this? You must work with this horse and say goodbye the right way, so that your mother can give him another life. You must spend some time with him and not just abandon him!" The young girl does not like to hear this. As they leave the ring, we hope that this horse will come to have the respect he deserves.

Another older woman comes to the ring with her horse. She loved horses but has no money whatsoever. Somehow someone gave her a horse for free and she has brought this mare because she is really new to horses. This mare and her new owner are lovely to watch, and it is clearly a match made in heaven. The horse loves her new owner and does everything she is asked—quietly, somberly, and with love. The trainer tells this lady that she will not have any trouble with this lovely horse and she should just keep working with her and all will be fine. It is the opposite scene from the one we watched before.

Then another beautiful woman who is in her early forties and has no children—she is the one who has arranged for this presentation on this huge horse farm—brings her horse, a magnificent paint horse. It is white and black and the lady is tall and stunning, fitting the horse perfectly, a great match. Then the drama unfolds. The trainer, again with her keen insight, says to the lady, "You are being too nice to this horse. He needs your direction, nice and clear; you must tell him what to do. You must be the boss." The lady is a very gentle and beautiful soul. We learned that at an earlier age she had suffered multiple burns all over her body, including her face. She was given this beautiful horse when she was young, and this horse had also been involved in a tragic accident when he was just a young colt. He was with his mother in a field and galloped into the middle of a prairie fire and was severely burned around his legs. Destiny being the way it is, here was a perfect match: both horse and rider had suffered enormously and now they were miraculously riding together. The trainer just pointed out a few things that needed to be practiced and they were on their way.

We watch a few more horses and their owners and it is time to go home. I drive home full of new ideas and enthusiasm for these beautiful beings, our friends the horses who have served us so well over millennia. I have spent the last month with horses, trainers, and shows, and I will try to apply what I have learned during these last few weeks. I have decided to go on a week-long ride in Wyoming on a horse ranch in August. Another plan is to go to Bolivia and ride out into the Altiplano for a month. There one can buy a horse and then sell it after the ride is finished. I had better hurry; otherwise I will be too old to undertake that adventure.

But here are some beautiful insights into the incredible horse from writer, painter, and esotericist Eleanor C. Merry who lived during Rudolf Steiner's time.

> The first use of horses as carriers of the soldier-guards, knights, or paladines of a ruler, was in the time of Akhenaten, Pharaoh of Egypt. This fact is really an indication, strange as it may appear, that the *consciousness* of the more advanced humanity was changing. The horse was the universal image in the mind of man of cleverness, intelligence, as against the old and fading inspired seership, or inherited clairvoyance. The symbol of the horse appearing in legend and myth denotes the approach of the "Twilight of the Gods". In the "Götterdämmerung," ... Siegfried and Brunnhilde appear, the former fully armed, and Brunnhilde leading her horse. Siegfried as *man*, without the old godlike clarity of wisdom but supported by human *intelligence*, is to plunge into the maelstrom of destiny.

Or, in Plutarch's *Isis and Osiris* we see how this change is suggested in the story of Osiris and Horus. Horus is seeking to avenge the murder of his father Osiris; and Osiris appearing to him from out of the Underworld, asks him what animal he thinks would help him best in his struggle against Set. And Horus replies: "The Lion is useful for him who is in need of help; but the horse is useful for pursuing and scattering the flying foe so that the battle may be ended utterly.[73]

She also mentions several coins which depict a horse from about the first century A.D. in England.

There is a variety of such horse-coins.... The horses of more ancient mythology were *heavenly* "astronomical" beings. The later ones are quite earthly; while the symbolic horses of the transitional time seem to have been a mixture of the two. For the [I]ntelligence was descending to the Earth, and the old star wisdom vanishing away.

The fifth century A.D. saw the first seeds sown in Britain of the Anglo-Saxon race, when Britain was invaded by *a mare and a horse*, the brothers Hengist and Horsa.[74]

Some of my questions regarding the future of the horse in our world deal with our changes in consciousness. When the horse suddenly appeared on the scene, as mentioned

73. Eleanor C. Merry, *The Flaming Door: The Mission of the Celtic Folk-Soul* (Edinburgh: Floris Books, l989), p. 148.

74. Ibid., pp. 149–150.

above, we were beginning to use our thinking, and the horse's appearance in our lives reflects this. We left our natural clairvoyance to enter the world of thoughts. Now that we are thinkers (at least some of us are) we are supposed to go back to clairvoyance but without giving up thinking. In fact, we are to use more of our thinking. What is the task of the horse now?

Could it be that these new methods that involve speaking the horse's language and becoming one with the horse reflect this new consciousness? They require being truly present, living in the animal world, and penetrating that barrier between "I versus it." We are becoming the horse's friend, caring for him as a little brother or sister, not his master.

Last week in England was the yearly ritual celebration of the opening of the horse racing season, a big gala affair where all the well-to-do aristocrats and nouveau riche go for days of champagne drinking, sumptuous eating, beautiful attire, large hats, fine horses, and impeccable manners, as well as gambling. The Queen issued an order that there would be guards at the door to make sure the ladies were dressed properly and with a hat; no one would be admitted past the appearance police if they displayed bellies or any other kind of flesh. No, we are not in Arabia, but Puritan England at its best. I must say I'd rather look at beautifully dressed women and well-dressed men than the usual scantily dressed young girls, which are more appropriate on the beaches of Brazil. I find I must agree with the Queen.

❦

I had to leave the farm at the most beautiful time when the gardens are magic, with irises blooming, peonies just opening up, and poppies doing their thing. I came back after a few weeks and it had gone by. It is like being taken away from your newborn baby. I nurtured the plants, endured back-breaking work and frenzied activities, and I missed it all. But never mind; now I am back at work, in full swing because it is haying time again. The weather is not cooperating and we are waiting out rain storms and more rain storms, and even tornadoes. We had 11 inches more rain than normal.

I want to dispel the notion that going back to the land is some sort of idyllic activity. Here is my schedule for the last few days:

Thursday: I am up at 6:30 in the morning to clean the kitchen, check on the chickens, and have a fast breakfast. A patient comes at 9:10 for painting therapy and leaves at 10:30. I then go to the garden and mow the alleys between the large flower gardens with the hand mower. It is hot and there are lots of mosquitoes. I have a fast lunch before doing more work outside, and make telephone calls to Spain, Holland, Massachusetts, and Alaska. Another patient comes at 4:00 for painting. I prepare supper, have the meal with my husband, do more gardening, gather the eggs and clean them— 10 days worth of eggs to be sold to friends. I read for a while and then go to bed.

Friday: I am up at 6:30 in the morning and indulge in a half an hour of reading. I check on the chickens, have breakfast of eggs and tea, do my emails, and deliver my eggs to the café owner. While I am here, I have a chat with a friend while it pours down rain outside—and on my hay field which has just been cut. Back home I do housework and occasionally watch the ominous clouds. At around 12:30 the sun peeks through the clouds, so I get on the little old tractor and bounce around through the field turning the hay, which has just been rained on. I have to stop several times because the tractor overheats and I must put some water in it. I finish at exactly 3:50, and see my patient heading for the gallery for her painting therapy session. She does not mind that I am quite dirty. We have our session, then she leaves at 5:00. I jump in the shower, throw some decent clothes on and head for downtown Milwaukee alone. My husband is on-call for 24 hours delivering babies. I have some Indian food and hear a great Brahms concert at the Symphony. I am home at 11:30.

Saturday: I am up at 6:30 in the morning. I check on the chickens, walk through the gardens to see who is there, get in the car and pick up milk at the farm, and swing by a friend's house to deliver eggs. Back at home, I get on the 60-year-old tractor. I turn the hay, which has been cut, so it can dry. One and a half hour later, I get on the big 50-year-old tractor with the combine attached to it and the hay wagon and pick up the hay. I have to stop every 10 minutes because the hay is getting stuck—up and down. It is 85 degrees and I am sweating and hot. I get off the tractor and onto the hay wagon parked next to the barn. I throw the 35-pound hay bales down so that my husband can put them on the conveyor belt to be thrown into the big old barn, and then I am back on the tractor. It is 4:30 and time to take a shower and then dress to go to Spring Green for an outdoor

Emptying the hay wagon

Shakespeare play—a two-and-a-half-hour drive. I am back home at 1:15 in the morning.

Sunday: I am up at 8:00 in the morning. I cook breakfast and make some very good tea just sent from Iran. I make butter from yesterday's whole milk, prepare the milk for yogurt, and take care of the eggs. Our small tractor is having difficulties so I can't turn the other side of the field that is full of cut hay. My husband is trying to fix it. The real mechanic is my son, but he is in Alaska fishing professionally for wild Salmon from his own old boat! I can't do anything until the tractor is fixed, so I get on my garden tractor to mow the lawn, since I have guests coming to look at my garden. No one understands what it takes to have a magic garden or a small farm—or what it takes to feed all the animals: 3 horses, 3 cows, 15 sheep, and around 30 chickens and 23 new chicks.

It is only 12:00 noon and we have another nine hours of work. I wonder sometimes how long I am going to keep going at this speed. I will be 60 years old in the fall and I can't see myself doing this when I am 70, which is only ten years from now. The rest of the day I need to get on the big tractor, bail the rest of the field, empty the wagons, cook supper, and do some editing here and there on a manuscript.

For now, I fix another cup of black tea and sit in the garden and vegetate for a half an hour or so. I listen for who is talking to me, the peonies or the yarrow. Actually it is the walnut tree which is saying, "Look at the little walnut trees growing around me." So I know that I have two little trees to plant somewhere nice. In the future people will need these trees to feed themselves. The nuts will be good gifts when nothing else grows. I read that somewhere in Rudolf Steiner's books.

From the big tractor out in the field yesterday, I could really see the grandfather tree by the studio-gallery standing tall and protectively overlooking our home. He is a beautiful tree, and I am so thankful that he is around. During the tornadoes last week he shed some enormous branches, which I cannot even lift, but they fell by the side of the gallery and missed hitting anything. I still have to clean the ground from all these fallen heavy branches.

As I bail the hay, the big machine breaks, and the northwestern skies are light-indigo, meaning a storm will be upon us within the hour. My husband is trying to fix it quickly, because the field still has lots of bales of hay which fell off the wagon and we need to pick them up. It looks like we won't be able to finish this job this afternoon. With more rain, there will be more turning the hay tomorrow. This year's haying is really a nightmare.

Back on the bailer I pray to the clouds, "Please drop your load on the neighbor's fields." They already hayed three days ago, thanks to their efficient $100,000 equipment. There is more trouble; this time the part of the bailer that picks up the hay is stuck. It works for a bit and then gets stuck again. The clouds are really moving in, and for my part, I look intensely back at the clouds to ask them, "Please, please, no rain just now." There is rain coming down just west of us, a whole wall of it, and a whole wall of rain north of us. Another problem: the big wonderful tractor has just stopped working as well. My first thought is that it is out of gas, and that would have been another disaster because it is a diesel tractor and if it runs out of gas, we need to wait a few hours before refueling or it will blow up.

Somehow the clouds are dropping their load on all sides of our fields and leaving us alone. But the thunder and lightening are crashing all around us. I would like some kind of enlightenment, but I don't want it that bad! To be struck by lightening is not on my agenda, so I run to the house while my husband tries to fix the tractor, completely oblivious to the storm.

I only had waffles for breakfast and I need some real food after lifting hay bails out of the wagon and dropping them on the conveyor belt. I also need to make a diesel gas run in the midst of this pandemonium. I am amazed that I can sit at the computer and write all of this in between happenings.

All the surrounding areas are having some nice rain, and in the middle of our fields we have some sunshine coming through a big break in the sky—a piece of blue sky surrounded by indigo showers.

... Rudolf Steiner spoke about meditations which the farmer should address to himself and the earth, and about beings which descend into the community of a farm and are active in the earth, the plants and the farm surroundings—and how then it would be possible for people to influence the weather by means of their moral-will forces. He spoke urgently about the degeneration of food-stuffs and how necessary it is to cultivate new plants. He also said that a whole new science should be established which would be effective not through itself but through esoteric realities....[75]

It is now 4:15, and there are only a couple of hours left before we must stop picking up the hay. Perhaps the clouds are actually listening to my pleadings! I think so. Now I must ask the elemental beings working so hard in our engines— three tractors in all—to please help us out. They must start working, and fast. As the reader can see, this is not the beautiful portrayal of country life in the garden magazines where everything runs smoothly, nothing breaks, and all is wonderful! I think the people in the magazines have an army of slaves to run everything. The idyllic, romantic vision of farm life is a fantasy.

It is now 7:00 in the evening. I have picked up the last row of hay, and all the bales are in the wagon, which will be emptied tomorrow. Then the rain starts, but it is a gentle rain; the big storm has passed us by and gone elsewhere. The tractors somehow work and I can have a well-earned rest, a lunch-coffee break-supper all rolled into one. My

75. Adalbert Graf von Keyserlingk, *The Birth of a New Agriculture: Koberwitz 1924 and the Introduction of Biodynamics* (London: Temple Lodge, 1999), pp. 66–67.

husband has to work again, all night. I hope the ladies will not be having too many babies tonight so he can get some sleep. I find I am too tired to cook, so I have some lettuce, an avocado, and bread for supper. That will have to do for today. The story does not end here; we have to start all over again in a few days, when another storm passes by and we can cut the other half of the field! Is anyone still interested in farming? Remember we both have other jobs as well, and we do not depend on the farm to make a living. You can see that the life of the farmer-gardener requires tremendous strength and sacrifice.

Two days later and I rise at 6:30 in the morning, jump out of bed and run to start the 350 pickup truck that we use to transport our horses when we ride in the parks. I drive it into the fields and pick up about 10 bales of hay that had fallen off. They weigh between 30 and 45 pounds, and they have to be lifted into the pickup truck. It is a little too much for my small frame even though I am stronger than I look. Consequently, I pull a muscle in my back and will have to put up with the pain for a few days. I should have warmed up instead of just jumping into action. I still have to unload one entire wagon with my husband who will get home late. Perhaps it will be too late because it is going to rain again.

One might ask how we came to live on a 60-acre farm. It all happened on a sunny, Saturday afternoon in the late spring. "Sold!" hollered the auctioneer to the Midwestern crowd, of farmers and friends gathered on the lawn of this old farm, the last homestead of the area. Hundreds of people were here to bet on this beautiful piece of land on a small country road 30 minutes from Milwaukee and two hours from Chicago. The bankers were here with the realtors trying to impress people with their money. They had parked their big expensive sports cars on the lawn as if to say, "We have the money, so don't bet; we will certainly out-bid you."

I had never participated in an auction before. We had seen the property the previous Thursday when my son saw an ad in the local paper saying, "Farm to be sold at auction on Saturday." We drove to it, saw it and fell in love with it, because it was just what I was looking for—not too big or small with a cherry tree in the backyard, which I interpreted as a sign that the place was for us. I need the sap from the cherry tree for my watercolor painting work. The property was a complete mess, but had outbuildings, an old dilapidated farmhouse and a small house which I could use as a painting studio. So we decided to bet on the property even though we really did not have the funds. We had purchased another five-acre farm down the road the year before, but that did not faze me. I got the $10,000 check that was needed to bet on the farm and decided to worry about the rest later.

The betting began and I found myself all at once excited, nervous, and enthusiastic. My husband let me handle all of it, and stood behind me with my son and daughter watching me over-betting myself. In the end it came down to one other fellow and me, and he finally gave up, seeing that I would not stop until I had the farm. We paid a bit more than expected.

Then I had to come up with the rest of the money. We went back home after giving them the check, and my son proceeded to make a huge "For Sale" sign which we put on the other farm's lawn so that it could be seen from the busy road. Within two hours a couple came with their eight children and offered us the price we asked, in cash. We

The old homestead

still have that sign in the shed. I now had the money to pay for the farm and we were in the new-old farm within two weeks. The banker in town, a very nice man, gave us a loan to cover our shortfall.

That is how we got to this farm. I guess when one is meant to have something or be somewhere, somehow one gets there through the help of friends and invisible threads, beings, and angels. We moved into a little one-room house while we completely demolished the old farmhouse. The boys went at it with pick axes and took out everything. Walls and ceilings came down, opening all the rooms, and we cut out large windows. The girls—me and my ten-year-old daughter—threw all the garbage into huge dumpsters we rented from a garbage removal company. We wore masks because of the dust, and my daughter and I spent days and days shoveling debris out of the windows. After more than three months of work, the house had only the original outer walls standing. We rebuilt it with new clean walls, new windows, and skylights in all the rooms, including the kitchen, bathrooms, and bedrooms. We had many arguments as to how to partition the new house. "I want the bathroom here," I screamed. "No, I want a larger bathroom here." "That is useless," I responded. "I only want one bathroom, and I want that other room for my office." It went on and on, but in the end they won. We have two bathrooms, but now the whole farmhouse is my office with stacks of books everywhere.

The final farmhouse turned out nice and light, with a woodstove in the middle of the dining-kitchen room. We painted all the walls, and moved in the first week of November. We were then able to take our first hot water shower since July. The kids really appreciated hot water after washing with cold water from a garden hose on the lawn for four months. They learned the hard way what luxury means—a warm small home with hot water. My son to this day thinks that he owns the farm, because he is the one who did all the carpentry, since his dad had to go to work. That is not bad for a 17-year-old. The day that we moved into the house from the cold studio was a celebration. My daughter and I had to go to our friend Ruth Zenniker's house for breakfast because it was so freezing cold we could not eat. We had slept badly all night trying to keep warm. During the entire summer, we used the lawn for our dining room, our kitchen, and washroom, and I had rented a porta-potty for a bathroom. People who came to visit looked at us with strange eyes. We must have seemed like gypsies with our things scattered about; I even had the table outside with a cloth and vase of flowers.

The author's son cutting posts and beams

During that summer, our horses (three of them, that we moved from the other farm) continually escaped because we did not have time to fix the fences. The chickens were not too happy in the old shed either, but in the end they got used to it. We were happy to spend time together rebuilding this farm. It gave the children invaluable experiences in appreciating what it takes to build something, and not to shy away from hard work. Many of the locals thought we were crazy and could not understand where our energy came from. We had no choice: it was rebuild, or live in a dump.

Now the children are gone and the farm is a little lonely, and the work of keeping the farm is sometimes beyond our capacities, as you may have noticed. As we get older, I wonder how long I will keep this up before I need to make some changes, as I must spend more time doing other work that is important to me. But I will always put my hands in the dirt to keep me healthy and humble. Collot d'Herbois once said to me during an interview: "You must be firmly on the earth if you want to do healing work! You can only heal if your feet are firmly planted on this earth, and not lost in the clouds!" And she also said, "Darling, when you paint, you can't do anything else, except cooking and gardening. Cooking and gardening and farming will not interfere with The Work!" I take that as great advice.

❧

The big barn has just been cleaned with a recently purchased Bobcat machine. It is easier than doing it by hand. We usually cannot find people to clean the barn with shovels, so now I have enormous piles of manure. I ordered some biodynamic preparations, which will arrive on Monday, and then I will spray some of the preparations around my gardens and put some on the huge manure pile.

The mosquitoes are ferocious. I cannot go into the gardens without a beekeeper's hat and without covering myself from head to toe. These mosquitoes have never been so fierce in all these years because of so much rain! I wish the birds would increase their consumption of these little pests. As I write this, a little hummingbird is coming for his snack, sitting on the feeder we have set up right in front of the window so we can watch them as we eat our meals. Regretfully, eating outdoors is impossible because of the mosquitoes. This is a shame because the garden room is my very favorite place in the summer.

A fast walk through the orchard and I see that the sour cherries are ready to be picked. I will make some pies and some jams this weekend before the numerous happy birds eat them. The peaches are not doing well because of the continuous rain and wind, but the plums are plentiful, and so are the apples and the pears. I need to mow the orchard. The tall grass is inviting to the clouds of mosquitoes that rise as I walk through it.

My early morning chores today include cleaning out the pond's filters and taking out the algae that grows there. Then I take 20 minutes before breakfast to weed the front garden where my Spanish roses grow, in full attire with the beekeeper's hat on my head, long pants and sleeves, and garden gloves. I bend down to pull the weeds, then I kneel, and wouldn't you know it, the mosquitoes bit right through my trousers. I got half a dozen mosquito bites on my behind! I can't win with these pests. I need to wear blue jeans now rather than thin pants.

We spend the morning taking care of the bees. We put on our new beekeeping outfits and smoke the bees so that we can take two supers from one of their busy hives. We have just run out of honey, but the hives are doing well. Now we have five of them, some busier than others. Aryan, the two-year-old gelding, stays close to us by the fence where the bees are, wanting to be part of the action, biting things, smelling things, imagining perhaps that he might be of help. He is curious just like a teenager. We check another hive that is new and not doing well, and discover that one of the boxes is mildewed and abandoned while the other two supers were doing fine. I hope that this beehive will make it; it is weaker than the others, probably because we did not clean out their boxes very well. The other beehive, which is by the chicken coop, is doing very well since we put in a new Queen, and they are multiplying and happy in their new home.

Taking care of the bees

Nowadays we take into account too short spans of time. In a recent discussion on beekeeping, for instance, an up-to-date beekeeper came out all in favor of breeding queens industrially, of selling the queens and distributing them widely, rather than having the individual beekeepers raise them themselves. I had to say: Of course, you are correct! But if not in thirty or forty years, then certainly in forty or fifty years you will find that this has ruined beekeeping.[76]

While my husband was extracting the honey, I picked up half a bucket of sour cherries. So for supper we can have cherry pie sweetened with new honey. Now is the time to send some gift packages to friends and relatives, with my

---

76. Steiner, *Agriculture*, p. 137.

mother at the top of the list. She is 86 and loves the honey! It does taste delicious; it is a miracle as always to taste the sweet flowing honey. I am always thanking these wonderful worker bees for the incredible amount of work they perform, peacefully sipping nectar from flower to flower all summer long. We will extract honey again in August, but will leave most of it for the bees to use themselves throughout the winter. I must say I also do my job for the bees with all these gardens full of beautiful flowers for them to sip.

The flower beds, however, are now full of weeds; I can't weed everything because my gardens are too large. I noticed that squirrels have been doing some mischief—highly beneficial mischief. They have been hiding the walnuts for their winter reserve and, of course, forgetting where they hid them. The results are little walnut trees growing everywhere in my garden among the perennials, which are tall this year because of the abundant rains. I did not pull the little trees out, so now I have dozens of baby walnut trees to dig up in the fall and plant as a new walnut grove. I will leave some in the garden, which in twenty years time will be different than it is today.

The walnut tree is beautiful to watch; its flowers are lovely, and the buds are some of the last ones to flower. The walnut is a slow-grower; it takes its time to absorb the sun and form this wonder-nut full of good oil; it's the olive tree of this northern latitude. My walnut tree grows next to a tall blue spruce—a little too close—and then there is a cherry tree a bit further away, so I can watch them stand together all year.

This land also has a large grove of hickory trees in the 20-acre meadow in the back of the property, sitting among the old oak trees. This area has a lot of strength; one can feel it. Perhaps this is the reason why I live here—to gather some of their strength so I can do so much work. Here is one of my favorite authors of meditation, Massimo Scaligero, from his book *La Luce* (The Light). This book is not easy to read, but it is full of wisdom approaching magic.

> We will need one day, to contemplate a tree, or a branch, or a flower with quiet intensity, if we want to discover the imaginative power of thought; if we want to attain, within ourselves, the thinking that edifies life. Such thinking is true only insofar as it is uplifting. By contrast, fixed abstract, and dialectical thinking ceases to be true.

> We need to cast our gaze onto the play of the light that rises before us as the form of a tree in order to see the movement of thinking that is born in us, from the depths of our souls, as the life of the very form that we are contemplating.[77]

> … [T]he art of the practitioner is to guide concentration to an intense purity without relying upon the brain's subtle forces or the tendency to evoke those forces to act upon the etheric body. Rather, the practitioner must act by means of etheric forces that are purer because of their independence from the etheric-physical system of the head.…

> … Each and every day, the ordinary work of thinking creates a wear and tear on the brain that one notices

---

77. Massimo Scaligero, *The Light (La Luce): An Introduction to Creative Imagination* (Great Barrington, MA: Lindisfarne Books, 2001), p. 76.

as tiredness. But, freed from their dependence on intellectualism, the etheric forces of thinking are truly inexhaustible.[78]

Another way to practice this is to read Rudolf Steiner's *Intuitive Thinking as a Spiritual Path* (also published as *A Philosophy of Freedom*).[79]

I go to pick some strawberries at the local CSA gardens this morning, one of my favorite activities this first week of July, while my husband is haying the other half of the field. We hope that the rain will go elsewhere. The other half of the meadow is nearly ready too, and my husband is turning the hay over, but the old tractor is once again acting up. He has been cleaning the fuel filter; diesel gas is not getting to the engine. The store is closed because today is the Fourth of July. There are more breakdowns as the day goes by and the result is that the field covered with hay will have to wait until tomorrow to be picked up. The store will be open then and I will have to make a run to Burlington, a 20 minutes drive—all this before having breakfast. Then I will have to pick up milk because it is Saturday. We have invited guests who will show up at 11:00 in the morning for an early lunch, although I do not know when I will have time to cook for them. I will have to throw together something, perhaps eggs, instead of the elaborate meal I had planned: Chinese meat balls. This is hamburger meat mixed with eggs, minced garlic, ginger, and other herbs dropped by the teaspoon into boiling water. They cook for at least 15 minutes, and then I add about two pounds of fresh organic spinach and cook

---

78. Ibid., pp. 80–81.

79. Rudolf Steiner, *Intuitive Thinking as a Spiritual Path* (Great Barrington, MA: SteinerBooks/Anthroposophic Press, 1995).

it for another 3 minutes. Then I make some udon spaghetti and serve them together. My guests with their two children are from China and I can't serve them Italian food as they would not like it.

On top of receiving our guests, we will have to finish picking up the field, about seven more loads of hay bales. In between now and tomorrow morning at 11:00, my husband will have to fix the tractor. Let us hope the elemental beings working in that tractor will help us.

✤

It is a beautiful Sunday with no rain and the tractor is fixed. The conveyor belt still breaks down here and there, but the hay barn is almost full of wonderful-smelling hay. One more wagon needs to be emptied and we are finished with hay for the summer. There will be enough bales to feed all the animals for another year—about 1800 bales, handled by hand. I think the animals know how much work we do for them, as they relax in the fields eating the fresh alfalfa and timothy grass. Now it is time to be off the tractor until next summer when I hope my son will do the haying and let me off the hook.

Meanwhile, my husband and I look like alley cats because we are both scratched and bruised from top to bottom because of the hay which easily cuts and because we always bump into the machinery while fixing it. This is in addition to the mosquito bites. I hope everything heals fast before our trip to Sweden. Scars do not enhance a cocktail dress.

The family from Peking has come and gone, and I never realized how much people are out of touch with life on the

The author's German shepherd

farm. The nine-year-old boy was a typical city kid, and his parents were typically urban as well. They had never been around a dog, never mind a huge German shepherd, and the boy was very upset, screaming and running around in fear. He also could not stand the insects, as he lives in an anti-septic apartment environment in Peking and Milwaukee. He never noticed the flowers or other plants, and walked among them as if they did not exist. He was even afraid of the flying bees, or going into the chicken coop. The food I cooked was not to their liking, so they left without eating. So much for my cross-cultural experiment. My husband has colleagues from all over the world, and I enjoy meeting them: Russians, Serbians, Poles, Thais, Africans, Indians and others, but this time the experience was depressing. We showed the boy tiny little birds from one of the many nests on the property, and he became upset because they pooped. He took pictures of everything, as if he could only see things through a window. It shows how separated he already is at such a young age. In the future this will mean a total lack of soul and warmth, and life. He will be like a robot that does as he is told without questioning. We are creating a very frightening world.

At another of our family gatherings we invited a colleague, his wife and his children—a boy and a girl from the Congo—and it was even worse. They were from a wealthy family and had absolutely no contact with any kind of animals. The visit to the chicken coop was a total fiasco. The girl became hysterical, as did her mother, who could not handle the chickens or the chicks. It seemed like they came to America, the land of plenty, to avoid any contact with manual work. That is for slaves, which they as wealthy Africans employ back in their own countries where it is not acceptable for an educated person to associate with such things. They think we are crazy to live in this manner when we have the means to sit pleasantly at home and do nothing except entertain ourselves with golf or tennis, or by going on expensive vacations. For a while we stopped inviting city doctors or folks from other countries to the farm.

A few years ago when my son was going to Maine Maritime Academy in the town of Castine, he invited a friend from Africa who was studying to be a sea captain. He spent a week with us, and was always upset with my son, and us, because in his eyes the son of a doctor should not do this kind of work and should always be dressed properly— my son wears rags—and then he looked at me. I told him my age, which was 54 at the time, and he did not think I looked like a grandma. He said that I ran fast, and it did not jibe to see a 55-year-old woman doing the work I do. We had fun with him, and he with us, even though ours was a world he did not really understand.

Now that haying is done, I have to put the Biodynamic preparations I just received on the pile of manure and spray the horn manure on a couple of acres after stirring it in the correct manner. I am a bit late in doing this, and I should have sprayed earlier in the season, but now is better than never. This year I will attempt again to fill the cow horns with manure. This is called the "horn-dung preparation" or "prep. 500." It is another gift from our friends the cows.

> Fresh cow manure is packed into the horn of a healthy cow that has fallen to the butcher's knife. In the fall, the horn is buried in good soil two feet under the ground and left until spring. After having spent the winter in the ground, the horn is taken out; the dung, by this time, is well-rotted and gives off a pleasant smell. One uses a pinch of this horn dung, about as much as a pea's size and puts it into a normal sized bucket of lukewarm rainwater. This is then stirred for one hour, preferably with the hand. The stirring is done in one direction until a funnel is created in the water, reaching to the bottom of the pail; then the direction is abruptly changed. Again a funnel is created, then the direction of the vortex is changed again and so on. Preparation 500, which aids rooting processes and terrestrial forces, is then sprayed....[80]

80. Storl, *Culture and Horticulture*, p. 345.

Stirring horn manure preparation

The spraying will be done tomorrow. Two more sour cherry trees are ready to be picked but I am leaving it to the birds or some friends. The plum trees will be ready in another month, and then the tomatoes, and the zucchini, and more. This night I gaze at the tiny crescent moon hanging low over the western skies, putting an end to a fine busy farm day.

The gelding Aryan was ridden with a saddle for the first time this week, and I have to ride the 18-year-old paint horse, old Silky, so that Aryan can copy her. This teaches him faster than simple training, and now that the field is cut we can teach him to follow the older mare. When he learns this new job, we can take him on weekend rides at the horse park close by. His mother China is doing a lot better, and perhaps will be able to carry a rider again after her awful injury.

Meanwhile we are getting frantic because in less than a week we are leaving the farm for a couple of weeks to visit relatives in Sweden. This week, therefore, I am the travel agent, the tour guide preparing our trip to visit Sweden and hike in Norway, the shopper for my daughter who has run out of "cute underwear," the gardener-priest, the housekeeper, cook, farmer, herbalist, therapist, wife, banker, investment specialist, writer, painter, scholar, and general caretaker.

❧

Finally, the long compost heap has been prepared with all the biodynamic preparations; I only have to sprinkle on the Valerian preparation. The big barn is now nice and clean, and all the manure will be ready to spread on the entire farm in the fall. I always enjoy putting these little spoons of magic preparation into holes on top of the manure piles, knowing that I am handling very fine forces. It is exhilarating, and I am always very thankful for the opportunity to rejuvenate our earth. In another couple of days we will be off to another continent. I will miss all of my beloved lilies, which will flower when I am away, and I hope that a few will wait until I return. A friend said to me the other day, "You will see other plants, so relax and have a vacation!"

When I am away from the farm, I always worry about the animals; they are always in the back of my mind. The dog gets lonely and starts to wander around, the elemental beings in the garden are abandoned because no one pays attention to them, and the bigger animals are left to themselves, although the old farmer does come to give them water. Food is abundant, but the chicks, which will hatch while we are away, will get lost, and some will die. A friend will come and gather the eggs. I must forget about the vegetable gardens. I worry the honey bees might swarm. How can I enjoy a vacation with all this on my mind?

When one truly lives with all these beings and gets attached to them, they become a part of one, and it is painful to leave them. Those of us on a farm are probably like the beehive, which is really an organism having a radius of several miles. I am truly part of this land and all these beings, and becoming separated from them is painful—for them as well as for me. However, one sometimes has other duties such as this trip to Sweden to meet my husband's younger brother whom we have not seen in 25 years. He can only take time off in the summer.

Winter is greatly appreciated here in the northern countries by people who work with the earth. It is time to rest—like nature—time to be stark, naked, and back to basics. We are like the gesture of seeds awaiting the spring, all tightly held together with intense power. And so it goes with life on the farm.

I will end with a little advice which Rudolf Steiner gave to a young couple who was interested in healing and working with nature spirits.

> You are both to go every morning, at the same time, to the same place, where there are meadows, trees and water. Observe a certain place—always the same one—under all conditions of weather. Make a change of location at the most only between summer and winter. Study the trees there and the shrubs and grasses, the forms of the clouds, the shadows and the rays of the sun on the leaves every morning.

After your observation do your meditation about the 'healing spirits.' And what you then have to try to do is to look at the plants, not by abstract study, but with living observation. The shapes of the roots, stalks and blossoms must speak to you—the plant must reveal its inner nature to you! Include in this the movement of the leaves, of the stalks and even of the roots....

Or the foxglove, what does it do? Its fine, loose roots are able to sink deeply into the earth as a result of the rain. Then it develops a very tall stalk which rises quite beyond the earth's gravity. And at last come the bell-like blossoms which again bend toward the earth: can one not see imaginatively how the foxglove expresses a state of equilibrium—first uniting in its roots with the force of gravity, then striving upward like an erect candle and, in spite of bearing the weight of the blossoms, reaching out toward the light; but turning again toward the earth with its blossoms. Can one not see by looking at it that it must have a harmonizing effect on the heart, alternatively uniting itself with gravity and then with the sun, and keeping itself in harmonious balance? In this way meditation must become a reality! Sulphur and salt, with mercury in between, work and become a reality. In this way one unites oneself with the basic elements of the plant's existence![81]

---

81. Keyserlingk, *The Birth of a New Agriculture,* p. 146.

References

Blatchford, Claire. *Friend of My Heart: Meeting Christ in Everyday Life*. Great Barrington, MA: Lindisfarne Books, 1999.

Cadogan, Susan. *The Community Cooks*. Townsend, MA: Amazon Publications, 1990.

Fitzgerald, Astrid. *An Artist's Book of Inspiration: A Collection of Thoughts on Art, Artists, and Creativity*. Great Barrington, MA: Lindisfarne Books, 1996.

Hauschka, Rudolf. *The Nature of Substance: Spirit and Matter*. London: Rudolf Steiner Press, 2002.

———. *Nutrition: A Holistic Approach*. East Essex: Sophia Books/ Rudolf Steiner Press, 2002.

Holt, Geraldene. *Recipes from a French Herb Garden*. NY: Simon and Schuster, 1989.

Keyserlingk, Adalbert Graf von. *The Birth of a New Agriculture: Koberwitz 1924 and the Introduction of Biodynamics*. London: Temple Lodge, 1999.

Klocek, Dennis. *Seeking Spirit Vision: Essays on Developing Imagination*. Fair Oaks, CA: Rudolf Steiner College Press, 1998.

Lipson, Michael. *Stairway of Surprise: Six Steps to a Creative Life*. Great Barrington, MA: Anthroposophic Press, 2002.

Lusseyran, Jacques. *Against the Pollution of the I: Selected Writings of Jacques Lusseyran*. Sandpoint, ID: Morning Light Press, 2006.

———. *Contre la Pollution du Moi*. Paris: Triades-Solear, 1992.

Magic and Medicine of Plants: A Practical Guide to Science, History, Folklore, and Everyday Uses of Medicinal Plants. Pleasantville, NY: Reader's Digest Association, 1986.

Merry, Eleanor C. *The Flaming Door: The Mission of the Celtic Folk-Soul*. Edinburgh: Floris Books, 1989.

Murray, Michael T. *The Healing Power of Herbs*. Roseville, CA: Prima Publishing, 1992.

Philbrick, Helen, and Richard Gregg. *Companion Plants and How to Use Them*. Kimberton, PA: Biodynamic Farming and Gardening Association, 2008.

Pickles, Sheila. *The Language of Flowers: Penhaligon's Scented Treasury of Verse and Prose*. NY: Harmony Books, 1990.

Proctor, Peter with Gillian Cole. *Grasp the Nettle: Making Biodynamic Farming and Gardening Work*. New Zealand: Random House, 2004.

Radin, Paul. *The Story of the American Indian*. New York: Liveright Publishing Corporation, 1944.

Remer, Nicolaus. *Laws of Life in Agriculture*. Wyoming, RI: Biodynamic Literature, 1995.

Roschl-Lehrs, Maria. *The Second Man in Us*. Canterbury, UK: Henry Goulden Books, 1977.

Scaligero, Massimo. *The Light (La Luce): An Introduction to Creative Imagination*. Great Barrington, MA: Lindisfarne Books, 2001.

Shakespeare, William, "A Midsummer Night's Dream" Act IV, Scene 1. In *The Complete Works of William Shakespeare: Gathered into One Volume*. NY: Oxford University Press, n.d.

Steiner, Rudolf. *Agriculture: Spiritual Foundations for the Renewal of Agriculture*. Kimberton, PA: Biodynamic Farming and Gardening Association, 1993.

———. *Bees: Lectures by Rudolf Steiner*, Lecture in Dornach February 3, 1923. Great Barrington, MA: Anthroposophic Press, 1998.

———. *The Bridge Between Universal Spirituality and the Physical Constitution of Man*. Great Barrington, MA: SteinerBooks, 1958.

———. *The Four Seasons and the Archangels: Experience of the Course of the Year in Four Cosmic Imaginations*. London: Rudolf Steiner Press, 1996.

———. *Harmony of the Creative Word: The Human Being and the Elemental, Animal, Plant, and Mineral Kingdoms*. London: Rudolf Steiner Press, 2001.

———. *The Inner Nature of Man and Our Life Between Death and Rebirth*. London: Rudolf Steiner Press, 1994.

———. *Intuitive Thinking as a Spiritual Path*. Great Barrington, MA: SteinerBooks/Anthroposophic Press, 1995.

———. *Learning to See into the Spiritual World: Lectures to the Workers at the Goetheanum*. Great Barrington, MA: SteinerBooks/Anthroposophic Press, 2009 [1990].

———. *Man and the World of the Stars: The Spiritual Communion of Mankind*. Great Barrington, MA: SteinerBooks/Anthroposophic Press, 1963.

———. *The Mystery of the Trinity and the Mission of the Spirit*, Lecture in Dornach July 28, 1922. Hudson, NY: Anthroposophic Press, 1991.

———. *The Social Future*, Lecture in Zurich October 1919. Hudson, NY: Anthroposophic Press, 1972.

———. *Spiritual Science as a Foundation for Social Forms*. Great Barrington, MA: SteinerBooks, 1986.

Storl, Wolf D. *Culture and Horticulture: A Philosophy of Gardening*. Wyoming, RI: Bio-Dynamic Literature, 2000.

Tucker, Linda. *The Mystery of the White Lions*. Mapumulanga, S.A.: Npenvu Press, 2003.

Whicher, Olive. *Sunspace: Science at a Threshold of Spiritual Understanding*. London: Rudolf Steiner Press, 1989.